PRAISE FO

"Dana Kaye doesn't just cor... box PR campaigns; she has th ...ecute them. Her understanding of the publishing industry, combined with her strong work ethic, make her one of the best publicists in the business."

—James Rollins, #1 *New York Times* bestselling author

"There's a reason I didn't hire an outside publicist through my first ten books. It's because I hadn't yet met Dana. Smart, no-nonsense, creative, and to the point, she's the best in the business. And you lucky readers get to hire her for only $16.99."

—Gregg Hurwitz, *New York Times* and *USA Today* bestselling author of *Orphan X*

"I wholeheartedly recommend Dana Kaye's *Your Book, Your Brand*. In the years I've known and worked with Dana, her ideas and strategies have been pragmatic, effective and cost efficient. I count her as an amazing and essential resource for my clients and the agency. I plan to buy this book by the carton and distribute it not just to clients but to my writer friends as well."

—Janet Reid, agent at Fine Print Literary

"When it comes to professionalism, hard work and dedication, Dana is the best there is! She has been invaluable in helping me build my brand, and has come up with really inventive ways to promote my books (like fun contests, which help me not only promote my books but also connect with my fans!)"

—Liz Climo, author and illustrator of *Lobster Is the Best Medicine* and *Rory the Dinosaur*

YOUR BOOK, YOUR BRAND

The Step-By-Step Guide to Launching
Your Book and Boosting Your Sales

DANA KAYE

DIVERSIONBOOKS

Diversion Books
A Division of Diversion Publishing Corp.
443 Park Avenue South, Suite 1008
New York, New York 10016
www.DiversionBooks.com

For more information, email info@diversionbooks.com

First Diversion Books edition September 2016.
Print ISBN: 978-1-68230-380-1
eBook ISBN: 978-1-68230-379-5

CONTENTS

For N^2

More than life.

For N^2

More than life.

INTRODUCTION

There is no magic to book promotion. There's no secret formula to creating a successful book, and it doesn't always take millions of dollars to generate a bestseller. You don't need a huge Rolodex of media contacts, large advertising budgets, or the full support of a Big Five publisher to make your book a success. While all of those elements certainly can help, I believe that every book, with the right strategy and promotional campaign, has the opportunity to sell well, including yours.

I don't have a public relations background. My college degree is not in business communications or marketing. I never worked for a publishing house or large PR firm. My first job in publicity was in 2009, when I took on my first client and named my business Kaye Publicity. At the time, I was just a 25-year-old freelance writer and book critic with some big ideas about how to promote books more effectively. As a reviewer, I received pitches from publicists on a daily basis. Some would send boxes of unsolicited books, others would send generic mass emails; some would send me personalized pitches, and the best ones always followed up. I started paying attention to why I picked certain books over others, why editors accepted certain pitches I offered them over others, and most importantly, what sort of publicity efforts resulted in book coverage, and which were ignored.

That year, at a mystery writers' conference, then-debut author Jamie Freveletti told me she was thinking of hiring an outside publicist for her first novel, *Running from the Devil*. I quickly gave her all my insights into working with publicists and a list of questions she should ask before hiring anybody. After writing down dozens of pointers, she finally just looked at me and said, "Why don't you just be my publicist?"

I became a book critic because I love telling people what to read and introducing them to new books. As a book critic, there were only two ways to do that: to write about the book for a publication or post a review on my blog. But as a publicist, I realized, I could do so much more. I could help authors improve their social media effectiveness, attempt to secure corporate partnerships, schedule and promote their book tour, and look for media outlets outside of the books sections of publications to talk about upcoming titles. Due to my experiences as a writer and critic, I had gained insight into what steps were necessary to secure media coverage, and what sort of publicist I wanted to be.

Through trial and error, I learned what works and what doesn't. Through hours of research, I gained knowledge of new trends and discovered which new technologies and marketing initiatives were worth paying attention to. I learned how to be a book publicist in real time, and this book is an opportunity for me to pass that knowledge along to you.

WHO HIRES A BOOK PUBLICIST? AND WHY?

If you're contracted through a small independent publisher with a limited staff, you may not have more than the bare minimum of in-house support. And if you're self-publishing, all promotional responsibilities fall on your shoulders. Though this means more work on your part to make the book a success, it doesn't mean it's impossible. There are many authors who are very successful in the world of self-publishing; some have even launched themselves onto the *New York Times* or *USA Today* bestseller lists.

But that's just for authors who are with small houses or publishing on their own, right? Why would an author who's signed with a Big Five house want to hire an outside publicist anyway? Big publishers, like all big companies, have a specific way of doing things. They have processes in place, budgets to consider, policies and procedures that must be followed. Their publicists do the best they can to secure media coverage, but they are overworked, underpaid, and have minimal support. I have teamed up with so many talented in-house publicists who just don't have the budget or the bandwidth to generate creative PR strategies or implement more tailored outreach plans. Many authors hire outside publicists to pick up where their inside publicists leave off and execute promotions outside of the publishers' budgets.

Many self-published authors hire outside publicists, marketing companies, or assistants to help them with the work load, but even more do it all on their own. And let's face it—not everyone has the budget to hire an outside PR team to supplement their publisher's efforts or to design a plan from scratch. That's where you come in. Whether you've got a lead title with a Big Five publisher, have signed with a small academic press, or are planning on self-publishing, this book will arm you with the tools you need to be your own publicist. After reading this book, you will have a clear understanding of your author brand and how to build that brand using traditional and online publicity, as well as utilize social media and in-person networking. You will know exactly what you have to do from the time you sign your contract to the day your book hits the shelves.

A common theme I will stress throughout this book is the importance of knowing your audience. I do not believe in media for media's sake or throwing a bunch of stuff against the wall to see what sticks. Once you understand your target and secondary audiences, all promotional efforts should reach those communities. I talk to many authors who constantly ask, "What about this? Or this?" to which I always reply, "Does it reach your target audience?" If the answer is no, then it's not worth your time. Not all media opportunities are worth pursuing. And many times, your efforts are far better spent elsewhere.

I also believe in keeping your eyes on your own paper. Focusing on what everyone else is doing usually does more harm than good. You constantly second guess yourself and worry that you're not doing enough. While I recommend that—as you're formulating your own PR plan—you observe what other authors are doing and gauge which efforts appeared to be successful and which didn't, or ask author friends who write similar books as you what worked and what didn't, you should do those things well in advance of your pub date. Once you formulate your own promotional plan, you should stick to it. As your pub date nears, you will get more and more anxious, and anxious people seldom make rational decisions.

The last point to emphasize is that book promotion is more of an art than a science. What works for one author may not work for another, and what's successful now may not get results in a year or two. In providing the tools outlined in these chapters, I strive to cover all types of books—traditionally published and self-published, fiction and nonfiction, e-only and print. This manual will guide you to choose the promotional tools that will best serve you and your book, but it's up to you to constantly evaluate what's effective and what's not. With your first campaign, you will create a media list and social media strategy, and identify additional marketing efforts that may work well for this title. As the campaign is executed, pay attention to which efforts are generating traffic to your website or which media outlets are the most responsive to your pitches. Take notes. When promotional endeavors hit or media coverage comes out, watch your website traffic, your sales ranking—whatever could indicate the promotion's effects. Take more notes. Then, when you get ready to publicize your next book, you'll know which strategies to replicate and which to skip.

BRANDING

WHY IS BRANDING IMPORTANT?

Almost every author I've met, whether they write literary fiction for a small press or category romances for Harlequin, has considered themselves an artist of some sort, and no one wants to equate selling their art to selling Kellogg's or Coca-Cola. They don't view their books as commercial products. But the purpose of branding is the same whether you're selling books or breakfast cereal: to let customers know what they're going to get before they buy. When you pick up a Coke, you know exactly what the soda is going to taste like. You know that the Lexus will have more luxury features than the Hyundai. When you pick up the latest Nora Roberts novel at the grocery store or a James Patterson book at the airport, you know what types of stories are within those pages. Known brands are comfortable, familiar, and come with limited risk.

According to Bowker[1], millions of books were published in 2013, and the majority of books purchased come from established bestsellers. While some readers are willing to take a chance on a new author or a book they've never heard of, most want a guarantee that the next book they pick up is worth their time and money. So, they go for established names (Patterson, Roberts), books that are getting tons of media attention (*Gone Girl, Girl on the Train*), or the current award winners (*Brown Girl Dreaming, All the Light We Cannot See*).

So what does that mean for new or midlist authors? How can you get readers' attention and build an audience in such a crowded marketplace? By establishing a brand.

Through a combination of publicity and marketing efforts, you will teach people what to expect from you and your books. Your social media content, the topics you speak about at conferences or discuss in media interviews, articles you write for websites or magazines—they should all reinforce this brand. You teach people, namely readers, what sort of content to expect from you. Then, when you have a new book out, readers are more likely to buy it because the risk has been reduced.

Think about the last 10 books you've purchased. Why did you buy those? Chances are, you bought those books for one of two reasons:

1. You're already a fan of the author and they have a new book out.

---

1   "Traditional Print Book Production Dipped Slightly in 2013," Bowker, Last modified August 5, 2014, http://www.bowker.com/news/2014/Traditional-Print-Book-Production-Dipped-Slightly-in-2013.html. See also the Digital Book World and Writer's Digest 2014 Survey of Authors.

2. Multiple friends had recommended the book, you've heard a lot about it on social media, and/or the book has received a lot of media attention.

I would bet good money that very few of you bought a book because you were browsing shelves alphabetically in a store, pulled out a book by an author you'd never heard of, read the back cover copy or the first few pages, and were sold. You wouldn't want to risk your time and money on something that hasn't been vetted.

Not only is branding crucial to selling books to readers, but it's also a necessary step to getting your book published in the first place. Like readers, publishers are risk averse. They want to know there is an audience for all manuscripts they acquire and evidence the book is going to be a bestseller. Publishers will look at your social media platforms, your previous publications, your presence in the community, and any public appearances you might have made. If you build your audience and establish your brand prior to the book's publication, you're demonstrating that you have a following and assuring the publisher that there is a readership for your book. Having an established brand makes you a less risky, more stable investment.

If you think of it, even the most creative, famous artists had their unique brands. Jackson Pollock was the splatter paint guy. Pablo Picasso was the guy who loved blue, cubes, and young, attractive women. The Beach Boys were fun and upbeat, while Bob Dylan was edgy and brought attention to social issues. Hemingway wrote "men's books" and loved adventure. Salinger wrote about young people and their relationships, while living as a complete recluse. Identifying and exploiting your own brand does not make you a sellout; it makes you savvy.

Gone are the days where you can be a Salinger-esque, reclusive writer, never answering fan mail and refusing to venture out to bookstores to do appearances. Authors are expected to be public figures, engage with their followers both online and offline, and provide their readers a sneak peek into their personal lives. Readers buy books because they like the author just as much as they buy books for the back cover copy or a quality review. If readers are interested in what you have to say, whether they hear you speak at an event or engage with you online, they are more likely to pick up one of your books. The digital age makes everyone more accessible, so your public persona is more important than ever for winning over readers.

THE CAVEAT

The first step is to always write a good book. Without this step, your branding campaign will be worthless. Many writers are so focused on marketing and publicity that they forget this crucial step. You can have the most comprehensive publicity campaign, sink thousands of dollars into advertising and marketing, and drive around the country doing bookstore and library events, but it won't mean anything if no one enjoys reading it. The idea is to hook readers and keep them coming back book after book, and they won't do that if you're not delivering a quality product. There's a reason people buy a Snickers bar rather than a generic chocolate bar: they know it tastes good.

If you're reading this book, but still writing your first book, then put this one down right away. Go sit in your chair, pull up your manuscript on your computer, and get to work. Write the book you need to write, without all the marketing and promotion talk clouding your process. Finish your book, then come back to this one. Without a finished product, you'll have nothing to market, and if it isn't high quality, readers won't keep coming back.

CREATING YOUR AUTHOR BRAND

The basic equation is fairly simple: You + Your Book = Your Brand. Your brand consists of who you are and what you write. Most authors we work with have one of two problems: they either don't see all the interesting parts of themselves that also relate to their book or they think everything about their life is interesting and is a part of their brand, even if it doesn't tie in to their book. It's necessary to take a step back and view yourself through an outsider's lens. You may not think that your degree in clinical psychology is a part of your brand, but if you write psychological thrillers, it definitely is. You may breed German Shepherds for a living, but if you're writing science fiction, that fact is not relevant to your brand.

For most of you, the "Your Book" piece of the equation will be easy, especially if this is your first book, if you write series novels, or if you've written multiple books in the same genre. Common denominators make the "Your Book" part a lot easier. But as I said earlier, you're an artist. There are many things that take your attention, and chances are, over the course of your career, you will write many different types of books. That doesn't make establishing a brand impossible, just slightly trickier.

Established Author Brands

Perhaps the best way to clearly understand what an author brand is is to look at other authors who have succeeded at establishing their own. One of the first steps is to look at how an author presents themselves in public and interacts with their audience.

One author who does this well is David Sedaris. Sedaris is more than an author; he's a performer and storyteller. He spent years building his audience on NPR and honing his storytelling skills performing on college campuses. He can also be awkward, but that self-deprecating humor onstage is reflected in what he writes in his essays, so again, that's part of his brand. Some books are better enjoyed in the comfort of your living room, but Sedaris brings his writing to life onstage and gives his readers a reason to come out and see him.

Another author with a highly successful brand is Lee Child. It helps that he's a tall, charming, attractive Englishman, but his success lies in his reputation for generosity and accessibility. He reads extensively and does his best to blurb upcoming books, especially those from debut authors. He regularly attends book festivals and conventions, and doesn't retreat to his hotel room directly after his presentation—he stays afterward to meet and talk with his readers and other authors. While he doesn't need to make live appearances at this point in career, he is committed to supporting independent booksellers, so he tours with every book he publishes. Readers support him because he supports the community.

Having a positive public persona and a favorable reputation is only a part of your brand: your book is the other. Saying that you write romance or mysteries isn't enough for your book to stand out on the shelves. You have to have a clear understanding of what you write and a short, concise way to convey that to your audience. Some quick examples include:

- Michael Crichton: High-concept thrillers that are based on scientific research and developments
- Augusten Burroughs: Dark memoirs veiled with humor
- Mary Roach: Investigative pieces into little known aspects of our anatomy and physiology

Not all books are this easy to classify and if you, like many authors, write in several genres and across many themes, you may be confused about how to classify yourself as an author. But never fear, there is always a way to create a brand that encompasses all that you write.

Finding the Common Denominator

While authors may think they write about many different topics and themes, in my experience, there are usually particular types of stories that authors are drawn to. Even the most prolific authors who write across multiple genres, age groups, and formats tend to gravitate toward certain story mechanics.

As an example, one of our clients, Sophie Littlefield, has written a small-town mystery series, a post-apocalyptic zombie trilogy, four paranormal YA novels, and now writes a cross between women's fiction and suspense. Most people would call her a branding nightmare; I called it a challenge.

Here are the descriptions for three of her novels:

A Bad Day for Sorry: Stella Hardesty dispatched her abusive husband with a wrench shortly before her fiftieth birthday. A few years later, she's so busy delivering home-style justice, helping other women deal with their own abusive husbands and boyfriends, that she's barely got time to run her sewing shop. Since Stella works outside of the law, she's free to do whatever it takes to be convincing—as long as she keeps her distance from the handsome devil of a local sheriff, Goat Jones.

When young mother Chrissy Shaw asks Stella for help with her no-good husband, Roy Dean, it looks like just another standard job. But then Chrissy's two-year-old son is taken, and Stella finds herself up against a much more formidable enemy.

Aftertime: The world is gone. And worse, so is her daughter.

Awakening in a bleak landscape as scarred as her body, Cass Dollar vaguely recalls surviving something terrible. Wearing unfamiliar clothes and having no idea how many days—or weeks—have passed, she slowly realizes the horrifying truth: Ruthie has vanished. And with her, nearly all of civilization. Where once-lush hills carried cars and commerce, the roads today see only cannibalistic Beaters—people turned hungry for human flesh by a government experiment gone wrong.

In a broken, barren California, Cass will undergo a harrowing quest to get her Ruthie back.

The Guilty One: Maris's safe suburban world was shattered the day her daughter was found murdered, presumably at the hands of the young woman's boyfriend. Her marriage crumbling, her routine shattered, Maris walks away from her pampered life as a Bay Area mom the day she receives a call from Ron, the father of her daughter's killer. Wracked with guilt over his son's actions (and his own possible contribution to them), he asks Maris a single question: should he jump?

At first glance, there are very few similarities between these three books. Three different genres, three different settings, and three distinct tones. But if you look closer, you can pick out a few common trends:

- Female protagonists, particularly single (or soon-to-be single) women of a certain age
- Missing or murdered children
- Stories of reinvention

Her agent and I worked together to take these common themes and come up with taglines we could use to discuss the breadth of Littlefield's work. Those included:

"Mothers doing the impossible to protect their children in the face of the unthinkable."

> "There is no cut deep enough to
> break the bonds of family."

These lines give you a clear idea of what Littlefield writes and who her target audience is, without focusing on one book in particular. It encapsulates all aspects of her writing and could apply to any of her titles. These taglines serve as the "Your Book" piece of the equation and serve as a jumping off point for the "You" part of her equation. Sophie is a mother of two, divorced, and has gone through multiple reinventions. She also worked in the tech industry, has a dog, and is originally from Missouri, and while these facts are interesting, they don't relate to the books, and therefore, aren't a part of her author brand.

Your Branding Worksheet

Now it's your turn! For each of your books, list the following:

1. Primary themes
2. Secondary themes
3. One line about the protagonist
4. Genre category

Once you have your complete list, circle or highlight similar answers. Use the answers that are consistent book to book to identify and shape your brand. Here's an example using Sophie's novels:

A Bad Day for Sorry

1. Vigilante getting justice for abused women
2. Being comfortable in one's own skin

3. Middle-aged overweight female who killed her abusive husband
4. Mystery

Aftertime

1. Surviving the apocalypse and rebuilding a new world
2. A mother overcomes every obstacle to find her daughter
3. Single mom
4. Post-apocalyptic thriller

The Guilty One

1. Coping with grief and moving forward
2. Does revenge equal justice?
3. Suburban mom trying to leave her husband
4. Women's fiction

Once you've identified the common trends, think about ways to combine those ideas and come up with 2–3 taglines you can use when talking about your work. These taglines don't have to be overly sales-y or sound like commercials. The goal is to convey the essence of your work in a short amount of time. Think of it as your elevator pitch, but instead of the pitch being for an individual book, you're pitching your body of work as a whole.

Some additional examples of author taglines include:

- C. J. Lyons: Thrillers with Heart
- Angela Scott: Books that Don't Bite, But the Characters Might
- Reed Farrel Coleman: Hardboiled Poet

It takes practice and you may try out a few before you settle on one that works. Run them by your critique group, your friends and family, maybe even ask a few of your fans their thoughts. They're the ones who have read your books and may have some insight.

These taglines serve as a jumping off point. But slapping a tagline on your website and Facebook page doesn't establish your brand. If that's all it took, you'd be reading a pamphlet instead of a book right now. So let's take a look at how to make the most of it.

ESTABLISHING YOUR BRAND

Congratulations! You've identified your author brand! The only problem is that no one knows about it. Once you have a clear outline of who you are and what you write, you must establish that brand out in the world.

Online Platforms

The first step is what I call "getting your online house in order." When you Google yourself, what do you find? If you're a debut author, you'll probably find your deal announcement in *Publishers Weekly*, your book listing on Amazon, and maybe even an eBay listing for one of your advance reader copies. But if you're an established author, the first thing that should show up in your Google searches is your website.

All authors, regardless of audience, will need an

author website. This serves as your online business card, a place where readers, booksellers, and media pros can find information about you and your books.

You do need to have a professional looking website, but you don't need to spend thousands of dollars on a web designer to accomplish this. Thanks to companies like WordPress, Squarespace, and Wix, you can download free or affordable templates and create a high quality website without the help of a designer. If you're more established, have a deeper backlist, and have the budget to hire a professional, you'll be able to customize your website even more.

I'm an advocate for not doing something myself that I can hire a professional to do better, but not having the budget is no longer an excuse not to have a website. Your domain name costs around $10/year, hosting is $5–$10/month and usually includes free domain names, and thanks to those services I mentioned, you can download plenty of templates for free.

All websites should include the following:

- A homepage that showcases your latest book and clearly displays your social media buttons and newsletter sign-up information
- An "About" or "Bio" page that includes your author photo, a 100–150 word professional bio that event coordinators and journalists can easily copy and paste, and if you want, a longer, more verbose bio which showcases your personality and background
- A "Books" page which lists all your titles in reverse chronological order, along with the synopses,

praise, and buy links. If you write multiple series or genres, you may want different pages for each of those series.

- A "Contact" page that has a contact form and, if applicable, your agent and publisher information
- A mobile-optimized template. Google penalizes websites that do not display well on mobile devices, so if your designer is using custom HTML or you're using an older template, your website may not be optimized for mobile. Search "Google mobile friendly test" and you'll be taken to the site that tests your pages. Plug in every page of your website. If everything passes, great. If any of your pages fail, the site will tell you why and what you need to do to correct that. Make sure to fix those problems ASAP.
- An analytics tool (Google Analytics, Stat Counter) that will measure how many people visit your website, where they come from, and that they do once they get there. This is a key part of measuring the effectiveness of your promotional efforts.

These are the basics. If you have nothing else, you should at least have these assets.

If you do hire a designer, or are just more tech savvy than the average author, there are some more bells and whistles I recommend adding:

- Embed your Twitter or Facebook feed right on the homepage. This will ensure there is new content on the home page regularly, which helps with search engine optimization (SEO).

- If you're planning readings, speaking engagements, and other live appearances, I recommend adding an "Events" page and using a calendar plug-in. A Google calendar, WordPress calendar, or other plug-in will display your upcoming events in a consistent format and will automatically archive past events. This can also be a place where you showcase available workshops or book club questions.

- If you publish frequently or plan to do extensive media outreach around your book, add a "News" page to your site. When you get a new review, are nominated for an award, or start a new series, you can let your readers know.

- For most genres of nonfiction, it's helpful to also include a blog. Blogging is a way to attract new readers to your site and continue strengthening your platform. By writing about subjects relating to your book at least twice a month, you'll keep readers coming back to your website and continue building your authority as an author. If you write fiction, I only recommend blogging if you're passionate about it. Building an audience for your blog is an uphill battle that's not worth fighting for its own sake.

These are the nuts and bolts of what your website needs. Next, you must consider, based on your brand, what your website should *feel* like. Oftentimes, this is the trickiest part—and also where web designers come in handy. They're the artists and can often take key words and vague descriptions and create a visual representation. But you can still do it yourself with a little creativity and the help of your tagline and branding worksheet.

Start with a color palette. If you write dark mysteries, then you should opt for darker colors. If you write light beach reads, then your site should boast pastels and lighter earth tones. Look at your latest book cover images and use them as an inspiration for your color scheme.

If you write in multiple genres or for different age groups, consider creating different color representations for each section of your website. This will subconsciously tell readers which books are lighter and darker, which are for an older audience, and which are for a younger one.

Depending on the template you choose, you'll most likely include some type of imagery on your page, whether it's in the header or blended into the background. Consider images carefully; think about what each image conveys. A cup of tea or coffee indicates something peaceful and safe, while a broken window or door left open conveys something menacing. Avoid anything too literal (guns for your thriller series, shopping bags for your chick-lit novels) and feel free to obscure or darken your selected images into the background. You can also opt for designs rather than photography or other literal images. But no matter what you decide, always pay for your images through stock photo companies; never pull images from the web.

If you're feeling stuck or not sure which direction to go, check out some of your favorite authors' websites and see what choices they've made. Write down what you like and dislike, and take note of the general feeling their website exudes. This will serve as inspiration and help you refine your choices to create a website that accurately reflects you and your work.

In addition to your website, you also want to make sure your other online platforms are up to date. It's helpful to do a Google search to see what is coming up first and what's getting lost.

If your book is already up on Amazon, then you want to make sure your Amazon author page is updated with an official bio, headshot, and latest books. If the Twitter account you opened years ago and never did anything with shows up, then you need to log in and make sure your avatar, bio, and website are up to date. Whatever is out there and coming up in Google searches should be the most accurate and up-to-date information available.

We will outline your social media strategy in a later chapter and help you to identify the platforms that are most crucial to your brand. However, just because you don't need to use the platform now doesn't mean you won't need it in the future. That's why I recommend securing your handle and login for all social media platforms as soon as they become available. You wouldn't believe how many other Dana Kayes are out there; it's a good thing I secured my Twitter handle early.

Take a minute and create accounts for the following:

- Twitter
- Instagram
- Pinterest
- Facebook
- LinkedIn
- Reddit
- Tumblr
- YouTube
- Google+

You don't need to do anything with them yet, just secure a straightforward username or handle. For example, if your author name is John Smith, ideally, all your handles should be JohnSmith. Since it's a common name and probably taken, other options include John_Smith, JohnSmithBooks, JSmithBooks, and so on. On LinkedIn and Facebook, your name can be the same, but the unique link to your profile should match your other usernames. If your Twitter handle is @JohnSmithBooks, then your Facebook name can still be John Smith, but your unique link should be facebook.com/johnsmithbooks. No matter what you choose, your handles for all platforms should be the same, so readers can easily find you across all platforms.

Most likely, you will only use a handful of these platforms, but having the online real estate is key for search engine optimization and discoverability.

Identifying Your Target Audience

Next, you have to gain a clear understanding of who your audience is and the best ways to position your book to appear on their radar. You reach teen girls in a very different way from middle aged men. But understanding your audience is more than identifying their age and gender. You need to put yourself in their shoes to understand what they're looking for and how they get their information about what's happening in the world.

Let's go back to the Sophie Littlefield example. As we discovered in the previous chapter, she writes a variety of different books, but there are quite a few similarities. Not everyone who enjoys *The Guilty One* will enjoy *Aftertime*, but there is a large cross-section that will.

That cross-section is women ages 35–55. The majority

of romance novel buyers are women ages 30–54[2], but since her novels all have strong familial ties and domestic themes, it stands to reason that her readership would skew slightly older. Also, mothers with young children (most likely ages 30–35) will have less time to read and purchase books. Many of her readers are probably housewives and/or empty-nesters, ranging from upper-middle class to affluent. They have disposable income to buy books and the time to read them. The women at the younger end of the spectrum probably also read celeb magazines like *Us Weekly*[3] and *People*; the women on the other end still flip through *Redbook*[4] and *Better Homes & Gardens.*[5] They listen to NPR midday shows in the car while they run errands and occasionally have the local news on in the background while they get ready in the morning. They're on Facebook to keep up with their kids and friends from college; they occasionally browse Pinterest, but they don't use or understand Twitter. They're in book clubs, involved in philanthropic organizations, and if their kids are out of the house, they enjoy going out, even during the week.

Can you clearly see this reader? By having a well-defined understanding of who your audience is, you're able to successfully tailor your marketing efforts to reach that audience.

---

2   Nielsen Romance Buyer Survey, 2014: "Romance Reader Statistics," Romance Writers of America, Last modified 2014, https://www.rwa.org/p/cm/ld/fid=582.

3   Us Weekly 2015 Media Kit: "US Weekly Reader Profile – MRI Fall 2015," SRDS.com, Last modified December 16, 2015, http://srds.com/mediakits/UsWeekly-print/Demographics.html.

4   Redbook 2015 Media Kit: "Key Audience," RedbookMediaKit.com, Last modified Spring 2015, http://www.redbookmediakit.com/r5/showkiosk.asp?listing_id=4912229&category_id=18969.

5   Better Homes & Gardens 2016 Media Kit: "Women Readers," BHGMarketing.com, Last modified Fall 2015, http://bhgmarketing.com/research/research-women-mri.

This will be extra important when we move into the publicity and social media portions of the book. Many authors are so focused on covering *everything* that they forget they only have to cover the places where their audience is likely to be. Your local radio station may have you on, but if your target audience doesn't listen to the radio, you're not going to sell books.

To stay focused, answer the following questions:

1. Does your audience prefer print or e-books?
2. Where do they get their information (TV, radio, websites)?
3. What else do they read (newspapers, magazines, blogs)?
4. Where do they buy their books (online, grocery stores, chain bookstores)?
5. What social media platforms do they utilize (Facebook, Twitter, Tumblr, Pinterest, Instagram)?

There is a lot of information in the subsequent chapters about specific publicity and social media efforts, so keep this list handy so that it doesn't seem overwhelming. Just remind yourself that you only have to reach your target audience and that many publicity and marketing initiatives may not apply to you, which will make the task at hand seem less daunting.

Once you understand your brand and your target audience, it's important to align yourself—and your brand—with like-minded people. Think of it like tables at a high school cafeteria: if you're selling to the popular kids, you shouldn't sit with the geeks. And not only do you need to sit with the popular kids, but you need to connect with them, too. And just like in real life, you can develop some topics of conversation to break the ice.

Developing a Content Strategy

You know your brand, you know your target audience, and you're starting to learn where they get their information. The next step is to figure out what you're going to say.

Open a new document or take out a sheet of paper and write out your tagline or author brand description you created earlier. Then, start listing types of content you could post to social media that would fall in line with you and your brand.

If you're having trouble, start by using some of these prompts:

- Where does your book take place?
- What themes are covered in your book?
- What is the tone of your book?
- What research did you conduct to write your book?
- What current events relate to the themes and topics in your book?
- Where do you live?
- What is your day job or background?
- What do you do when you're not writing?
- Do you have kids? Pets?

Continue listing topics and types of contents you could post about until you have a list of 15–20. Now, go through and highlight the topics that meet the following criteria:

1. Topic relates to your author brand
2. Topic appeals to your target audience

Hopefully, you end up with a list of at least 10 topics you could potentially write about. To ensure you're on the right track, here is a list using Sophie Littlefield as an example:

Brand taglines:
- "Mothers doing the impossible to protect their children in the face of the unthinkable."
- "There is no cut deep enough to break the bonds of family."

Topics:
- Being a mother, life as a single mother, and other familial topics
- Books, movies, and TV shows with strong female characters
- Feminist topics
- Living in the Bay Area, Oakland in particular
- Notes about reinvention after divorce
- Living life after 50
- Writing and publishing
- Real-life vigilante justice
- Amazing mothers and their children

Each of these topics directly relates to Sophie's author brand and people who are interested in such topics would also be interested in her books.

This list of topics will later become your content strategy for social media, the talking points you send out with your media pitches, and the basis for talks and workshops you sign on for. We'll explain the different ways they'll be used in subsequent chapters.

As you get deeper into the publicity process, you may be asked to give a talk on a certain subject or weigh in on a news item for a newspaper or radio show, but should you accept if the topic doesn't appear on this list? Or if you have a strong opinion on a trending Twitter topic that's not on this list, is it okay for you engage in the conversation? We as people are more than our brands and have ideas and opinions that expand outside this seemingly limited scope. But once you signed that book deal or published your first book on your own, in that moment, you became a public figure. And as a public figure, going outside your author brand can have a negative impact.

I once had a client who earned a reputation of getting into altercations and heated discussions on Twitter. He wasn't an argumentative person, but when he saw internet trolls bullying authors or people from the Westboro Baptist Church bullying, well, everyone, he felt the need to step in and intervene. As a person, I completely understand that temptation, but as a public figure, it's not his place and it's not a part of his brand. His online altercations with these types of people—even though most would agree that he was on the side of angels—resulted in him losing followers and other authors distancing themselves from him. Which is a shame, because he is a terrific guy and a supremely talented author. He just needed to stay on brand.

Whether you're writing a blog post, giving an interview, or appearing at a bookstore, know your content strategy and stick do it. And most importantly, don't be afraid to turn down any interviews or appearances that aren't a part of your brand. It may be tempting to say yes to every opportunity, but despite popular opinion, not all publicity is good publicity.

RESOURCES

HOSTING

Dreamhost.com

Siteground.com

WEB TOOLS

Google's mobile friendly test

Wordpress.com

Wix.com

Squarespace.com

Weebly.com

Google.com/analytics

StateCounter.com

STOCK PHOTOS

iStockPhoto.com

DepositPhotos.com

TRADITIONAL MEDIA

INTRODUCTION

With so much emphasis on social media and digital marketing, it's easy to believe that traditional media is a thing of the past. Newspapers have been replaced with tablets, radio shows with podcasts, and live TV with streaming services. If you live in a city where most people rely on public transportation, you forget that in other parts of the country, people drive to work, probably with the local NPR affiliate or morning shock jocks playing. And while many Millennials have given up their TV, the Gen Xers still turn on TODAY or Good Morning America as they get ready for work. The landscape of traditional media and the way it's consumed may have changed, but it's hardly a thing of the past and remains an important facet of most successful campaigns.

Types of Traditional Media

All traditional media outlets fall into one of two categories:

print or broadcast. Print outlets can be further broken down into magazines and newspapers, and broadcast outlets into TV and radio. And those can be broken down even further.

Magazines

These magazines are distributed partially through subscriptions, the rest through in-store purchases, usually at grocery stores and pharmacies. For anything you're interested in, there is a monthly magazine. Whether it's knitting, bass fishing, or overcoming addiction, there is a publication out there suited to your interest. There are also location specific magazines highlighting attractions and people in certain cities or regions. There are also many trade publications, like *Publishers Weekly* or the *ABA Journal*, which are specific to certain industries. Even though print publications are on the decline, most magazines still have a wide enough distribution to make them worth pursuing for media coverage.

Daily newspapers

Nearly every city, town, and village has a local paper, albeit, some smaller than others. Most daily newspapers are sold through subscriptions, but some are still purchased at newsstands and in vending machines. Daily newspaper subscriptions have greatly declined, but coverage in your local paper still makes a difference. If you live in a bigger market like New York or LA, a feature in a local newspaper will reach a bigger audience. If you live in a smaller market, the rate of people who subscribe to the newspaper tends to be a bit higher because people want to know what's going on locally, so you still reach a captive audience. And if you live in a really small market, there's a great chance of people having already heard your name or being somewhat familiar with your work. A piece in the local paper could be the factor in turning you from someone they've heard of to someone they read.

Community newspapers and alternative weeklies

Community newspapers are specific to a certain neighborhood or market within a larger demographic region. For example, in Chicago the daily newspapers are the *Chicago Tribune* and the *Chicago Sun-Times*. But we also have the *Chicago Journal*, which covers the near south and west sides, and *Insider Chicago*, which covers a handful of neighborhoods on the north side of the city. While community newspapers tend to be neighborhood or location specific, alternative weeklies are broader. Some of these weekly newspapers are still independently owned and serve as the alternative news source to the big corporate newspapers, but many have been purchased by larger companies and have moved under the corporate umbrella. Examples of these papers include *LA Weekly*, *Chicago Reader*, *Creative Loafing*, and others. Most of them are free and tend to reach a younger demographic.

TV news shows

When it comes to pitching TV appearances, you'll mostly be pitching to the news shows. Most stations have a morning and evening news broadcast, and some also have a midday show. Most syndicate the national morning shows (TODAY, Good Morning America, etc.), but some stations produce their own (Fox's Good Day, WGN News). Some shows, usually the evening time slots, are all news and don't accommodate guests. You want to focus your attention on the shows that produce segments, cover lifestyle pieces, and host experts to discuss events in the current news cycle. These are usually the morning and midday shows.

There are also shows on the 24-hour news networks like CNN, Fox News, and MSNBC. Some of these shows will bring on experts or host segments, but others don't. All national shows can be difficult to book, especially if you've never done TV appearances before, but understanding the shows and what they cover will help you become more knowledgeable of the market as a whole.

TV talk shows

Rather than a news format, these shows revolve around interviews and lifestyle segments. There is usually one host who interviews a series of guests along with some on-site coverage. While the topics may revolve around something timely (a book release, political race, etc.), the talk shows are not the ones breaking news. They are planned and recorded ahead of time. Most of these shows are national (Ellen, The View, The Late Show), but there are some networks that produce their own. Again, the bigger the reach, the more difficult it is to book, so first focus on the local markets before shooting for the nationals.

Network radio

These shows can be broken down by national, regional, and local stations. The bigger the demographic, the further the reach. Most radio shows will interview guests over the phone, which is great because you can reach a market without actually setting foot in that state. There are talk radio shows which, like the TV talk shows, focus on guest interviews and commentary on current events rather than actually breaking the news about them. These are the shows to focus on because listeners tune in to hear people talk. There are also music stations that host interviews in between songs, but these aren't as effective because their listeners just want to hear music and often change the channel when they find out there's going to be 10–15 minutes of talk. Like other traditional media, the national shows are the most challenging to secure. Start small, focus on the local stations, then work your way up.

Satellite radio

While this technology officially launched in 2001, Satellite radio truly didn't gain popularity until 2008 with the formation of Sirius XM. Unlike network radio, which relies on advertisers to keep them in business, Sirius XM is a paid subscription that allows you to skip the ads and just listen to the music or programming you want. In addition to various music channels, there are also dozens of programming channels, ranging in topics from sports, to politics, to LGBT issues. Like monthly magazines, whatever you're interested in, Sirius XM has a station for you. And since there's more programming and less reliance on advertisers, there is more room for guest interviews.

Timing

When planning your traditional media outreach, it's important to factor in lead time; how far in advance media outlets plan their coverage. Most monthly magazines work on a 6–7 month lead time, meaning the right time to pitch your June book release is in December. By the end of January, the magazine will have closed its June issue. Daily newspapers or weekly publications have a shorter lead time, but if you're seeking review coverage, you have to factor in time for critics to read the book. TV and radio have a much shorter lead time, but if your dates aren't flexible, like if you're going to be in a particular city only the day of your event, you should give yourself an extra week or two to ensure you secure your slot.

While this shouldn't be taken as gospel, here are the basic guidelines for most media outlets:

- Monthly magazines: 6–7 months
- National TV and radio: 2–3 months
- Daily and weekly print publications: 6–8 weeks
- Local TV and radio: 2–4 weeks

Keep in mind that these guidelines are for pitching reviews and interviews where the primary focus is on your book. These feature stories, or fluff pieces, are scheduled further in advance than pieces pertaining to the current news cycle. There may be times when something happens in the world and you happen to be an expert on that topic (we'll address this further in the "Pitching" section of the book). In those instances, outreach should begin as soon as possible and can happen within the hour. When an American was gored at a bull running festival, CBS This Morning had a car picking up our elite bull-running client, Bill Hillmann, that night to take him to the local studio and discuss the topic. Breaking news trumps all coverage, and because stories develop so quickly, it requires little to no lead time.

Goals

When planning out a traditional media campaign, it's important to establish clear goals. If you're a novelist, your primary goal is probably book sales. If you write nonfiction, media appearances can help leverage speaking engagements or build a platform for their next book. If you're in academia, publishing op-eds and essays can help secure a new position or help build your profile in your university.

I've heard countless authors who tell me their goal is to "just get their name out there," and my response is always the same: why? What purpose does "getting your name out there" serve you if it's not directed at your target audience or going to result in book sales? I never advocate media for media's sake; all media appearances should aim to accomplish a goal.

In most cases, the goal is to sell books. Therefore, all media appearances should be directed at your target audience. If men are your primary book buyers, then appearing on Ellen or The View isn't going to help you. If you're a romance writer, then an op-ed in the *Wall Street Journal* isn't going to reach your readers. Once you start planning out your campaign and thinking of different ways to pitch you and your book, you may be surprised by how many opportunities are out there. But not all media opportunities are created equal. If it doesn't help accomplish your goal, then you're better off spending that time writing your next book or looking for a better opportunity.

Go back to the list you created in the previous chapter. Who is your target audience and where do they get their information? Use that list to evaluate media opportunities and focus your efforts. If your target audience doesn't read monthly magazines or watch the morning shows, then you shouldn't focus your efforts there. Picture your typical reader and imagine their typical day. Think about what shows they watch or listen to, if they read in print or on a device, if they read mainstream news sites or prefer more video- and image-driven sites. If you can't picture your reader, it's going to be difficult to market to them.

CREATING A MEDIA LIST

Using your answers from the branding questions as a guide, take a few moments to jot down every traditional media outlet your target audience may consume. These can be as broad as "local TV news" or as specific as "Fox & Friends." Don't worry about how hard these media outlets are to reach or if there's a way to pitch the interview. Just think about your typical reader and how they get their information.

Let's say you write business books and your target readers are those in high-level executive positions, or those who hope to rise to those positions in the near future. This reader is informed, probably a news junkie. Your reader could be male or female, though probably male, in his 40s–60s. He's still working, so the broadcast media he consumes is in the morning or later in the evening. He doesn't consume his media online, other than a few news sites and newspaper-based subscription services, but he probably travels for work, so he could still use an e-reader.

Take a minute and write down all the media outlets your typical reader consumes. Here is a sample media list, using the business book reader as an example:

- *Wall Street Journal*
- *New York Times*
- Fox News
- CNBC
- Morning Edition on NPR
- Local news talk radio
- *Inc.*
- *The Week*
- *Harvard Business Review*
- Local evening news

Once you have 10–15 outlets written down, identify any patterns. Can you identify the patterns in our sample list?

Once you identify the patterns of your list, expand it using other media your readers might consume. For example, if our target audience reads the national newspapers, chances are, they also read the local one too. While one member of our group may watch Fox News, there could be just as many people who would watch CNN.

Here is our expanded media list:

- *Wall Street Journal*
- *New York Times*
- *USA Today*
- *Washington Post*
- *Chicago Tribune*
- *Los Angeles Times*
- Fox news
- CNN
- MSNBC
- CNBC
- Morning Edition on NPR
- All Things Considered on NPR
- Diane Rehm
- *Inc.*
- *The Week*

- *Harvard Business Review*
- *Entrepreneur*
- *Newsweek*
- *Forbes*
- *Financial Times*
- *The Atlantic*

- Local paper (where author lives and/or where the book takes place)
- Local news talk radio
- Local evening news
- Local morning news

If your target audience is teenage girls or stay-at-home moms, your media list will look completely different. Don't be afraid to cast broad generalizations or use people in your life as examples. If your spouse fits the description of your typical reader, jot down all the things they read, watch, or listen to. If your friends or neighbors fit your description, don't be afraid to take a quick poll and find out where they get their information.

Additionally, keep in mind the tangential audience. If you're trying to reach teenagers, another way to do that is through their parents. If you're trying to reach older readers, another way to do that could be through librarians and booksellers since many older readers still prefer print books.

Finding the Contacts

Once you have your initial media list, you'll need to find the appropriate people to contact. There's a misconception that the rolodex of media contacts is something exclusively built by PR professionals and only they hold the key to securing media coverage. That's not true. Many producers and editors are happy to hear from authors directly (as long as they're approached in a professional manner), and their contact information is accessible to anyone. In reality, there are two ways to do this: buy a media database or do the research yourself. One way saves you a lot of time, but tends to be costly. The other is free, but can take up a lot of time.

Media Database

As a PR company, we reach out to media on a daily basis, so it makes sense for us to invest in a media database. These databases not only provide contact and background information for all media outlets in North America (or internationally, depending on your service), but they maintain that information so it's always up to date. Reporters and producers come and go on a regular basis and their assignments are frequently changing, so having a subscription to a media database saves a lot of time and research. However, they can be expensive ($2,000–$4,000 a year, depending on your plan). If you're planning on doing your own PR for multiple books, it may make sense for you and a few of your author friends to go in on one together.

Some of the most popular media databases used by PR pros:

- Cision – most widely used and most comprehensive—also the most expensive
- MyMediaInfo – a newer service—some say it's less comprehensive, but many are happy with it
- Robin 8 (formerly MyPRGenie) – a new service that relies on artificial intelligence to not only pull media contacts, but also freelancers and bloggers writing about certain topics

Do the research

If you don't have the budget for a media database or have the time do the legwork, contact information for most editors and producers can be found online. It just takes a little googling.

Start by going to the media outlet's website. Peruse the various sections and think about where coverage of you and your book would fit in. Does the publication have a "Books" section, or is it lumped into "Arts and Culture"? Does the radio show do on-air reviews? Guest segments? Knowing where you fit into the current coverage is the first step in identifying the appropriate contact. Also make notes if they've covered a similar book, published articles from guest contributors, or brought on guests for expert commentary.

With these notes in hand, look for the "About Us" or "Contact Us" page. Most print publications provide a detailed masthead. Try to find the most specific editor possible and then work back from there. If you're seeking a book review, your best contact is the "Books" editor. If there isn't a "Books" editor, look for the "Arts & Entertainment" or "Culture" editor. No dice? Then go for the features editor or even the managing editor if it's appropriate. Bigger publications have larger staffs, so you want to be as specific as possible, but smaller publications may only have a couple of editors, or even a sole editor in chief. If it's a small publication, there's no harm in contacting the editor in chief. The same is true for radio; at smaller stations, hosts book their own guests and produce their own shows. When finding the appropriate contact information, take the size of the outlet into consideration.

While many media outlets have the appropriate contact information readily available, there are others who make it a little more difficult for people to contact them. They will have contact forms or generic editor@publication.com email addresses. You shouldn't discount these options completely—at Kaye Publicity we've had plenty of successes pitching to generic email addresses if that's how the publishers have preferred to work, but since these sites probably receive thousands of emails at these addresses, I wouldn't assume that your message reached the appropriate person. In these instances, I recommend first emailing the generic address, then following up with a phone call to a specific editor. We'll address follow-ups in a later section, but in the meantime, make a note of the outlet's phone number.

On the rare occasion when there is no way to contact the person online, you'll have to pick up the phone. I know this is scary for most people, but trust me, good things come to those who call.

When you call the main line, chances are you'll be greeted by the operator or receptionist. Be friendly, say you're trying to get in touch with the books editor or the producer for a particular show. Hopefully, they'll connect you to the appropriate person, but it may take some bouncing around. Half the time, you'll be greeted by a voicemail. This is great because all you have to do is leave a short elevator pitch with the offer to send more details via email. Speak slowly, clearly, and leave your phone number and email address twice. If you do get a person, introduce yourself, say you were interested in sending them a pitch, and ask if they have an email address you can use. If they ask for your pitch on the phone, have your elevator pitch ready!

Doing the research definitely takes a lot more time, and it may be more difficult to get contact information for the bigger outlets. But that doesn't make it impossible.

There is no question that the pool of traditional media outlets, particularly those covering books, has shrunk dramatically over the last decade. If you spend most of your time with the millennial generation, it can be easy to view traditional media as obsolete. But traditional media still plays a role in most successful publicity campaigns. There are a few exceptions, but if you look at the books gracing the top ten bestseller lists, it will be hard to find any titles that haven't received some sort of traditional media coverage.

RESOURCES

MEDIA DATABASES

Cision.com

pr.robin8.com

MyMediaInfo.com

ONLINE MEDIA

INTRODUCTION

There's no question that media coverage is moving more and more online. In previous years, securing a *New York Times* review or an appearance on the TODAY show was every author's dream. Now, there are websites and blogs that have an even larger readership, and unlike newspapers, which are discarded each day, or morning shows, which are only available in the moment, online media coverage is available to be accessed forever (more or less). Traditional media should be a facet of most publicity campaigns, but it no longer determines a book's success. There have been hundreds of bestsellers that never received a single print review.

While some books can hit the bestseller list without traditional media coverage, I've never seen a successful book that didn't have an online component to the promotion strategy. Even older audiences read news sites and forward articles to friends. And if your audience skews younger, they're likely not watching the morning TV programs—your best shot at reaching them is through online outlets. Receiving a review on *Bustle* or *Newsmax* may not be as prestigious as a *New York Times* review, but prestige doesn't necessarily sell books.

There are many facets to online promotion, but in this section we will focus on online publicity, which is different from online marketing and social media. Publicity is securing editorial coverage of the book in the form of a review, interview, or other feature, and that's what we'll focus on in this section.

TYPES OF ONLINE OUTLETS

There are four major types of outlets that feature online publicity.

Websites

When it comes to structure, websites are most similar to newspapers and magazines. They are broken up into sections, have an editorial staff, and usually have a distinct mission or voice. The content is written by staff writers as well as guest contributors, which is then edited and curated by a staff of editors. Some smaller websites may be run by only a handful of people, while the larger ones have a staff of hundreds.

There are seemingly endless types of websites: news sites, lifestyle sites, sports sites, and the list goes on. Like magazines, think of anything that interests you and there's usually a website for that. For the purposes of this section, we are focusing on editorial sites, not those dedicated to a business, organization, or other form of e-commerce. The websites under discussion here are those with articles, interviews, quizzes, and other editorial content. Examples include *Huffington Post*, *Daily Beast*, *BuzzFeed*, *Hypable*, and others. This can also include the online components for popular print publications like the *New York Times* or *Seventeen*. Because the web provides endless space for content, many articles and features which don't make it into the print publication will often appear on the website.

Blogs

Unlike websites, blogs do not have an editorial staff, and the content is written by one writer or a group of writers. The voice is based on the person writing the content rather than the editorial voice of the publication. Many newspapers and magazines have blog components, which are run by individual staff writers or editors. These are structured like columns and take on the voice of the columnist.

It is usually fairly easy to differentiate a blog from a website by looking at the "Contact" or "About Us" pages. There, you should clearly see who is writing the content and whether or not there is an editorial process. If it's not clear, take a look at the articles posted. Are they all written by the same person or the same group of people? Are there different sections of the site or is it one stream of content? If the content is broken up into sections and there are many different writers posting content, then there's a good chance you have a website, not a blog.

The differentiation between the two is important for a few reasons. First, understanding the structure of the media outlet will help you understand how and to whom to pitch. A website deals with editorial content in a different way than an individual blogger. This will be addressed further in the "Pitching" section.

Second, there is a different editorial standard and code of ethics for websites and blogs. Unless the blog is curated by a newspaper or larger publication, it's usually run by an amateur who often isn't familiar with the standards and ethics of journalism. They are not obligated to fact check or cite sources, and the content is largely based in opinion rather than presentation of facts. You cannot assume they will double check quotes from your book, fact check your bio, or only present data with proper citation. I work with many bloggers who are former journalists and are extremely professional when it comes to disclosing sample products, pulling photos from the web, and quoting their interview subjects properly. But there are many more who aren't familiar with those practices. I recommend treading lightly when it comes to participating in phone interviews, which may leave you open to being misquoted, and be prepared when you send off your book because they may get certain facts wrong, and some may not even read the whole book before posting their review.

This is not to say that blogs are not worth pitching to—they are. There are many influential bloggers who have large followings and are able to effectively promote your work. But the expectation for the reader should be a bit different. An interview or feature on a blog may not be held to the same editorial standards as one on a news or lifestyle website. Any outlet with an editorial team will be held to a higher standard; therefore reviews or features on those sites will hold more clout. Clout is different than influence. Sally's book blog may have more subscribers and influence than the *Los Angeles Review of Books*, but she doesn't have the same clout.

Podcasts

These are online radio shows, usually available for download through iTunes, Google Play, or the individual's blog and website. A few years ago, podcasts were these obscure shows produced by amateurs in their basements that only hipsters and more tech-savvy people listened to. But now that no one ever leaves home without his or her phone, the popularity of podcasts has increased dramatically. Popular sports talk radio podcasts are being downloaded in the hundreds of thousands, and NPR's breakout hit, "Serial," has been downloaded or streamed more than 5 million times.[6] These days, most mainstream radio shows produce supplemental podcasts, and even many amateurs have upped their production game and managed to secure a following.

Like traditional media, the bigger and more popular the show, the harder it is to land coverage there. But you also don't want to spend time doing an interview on a poorly produced show with no following. Listen to podcasts, read their reviews on iTunes or Google Play, look at how many times they've been downloaded. It will be easy to distinguish the pros from the rookies.

---

6   David Carr, "'Serial,' Podcasting's First Breakout Hit, Sets Stage for More," *New York Times*, November 23, 2014, http://www.nytimes.com/2014/11/24/business/media/serial-podcastings-first-breakout-hit-sets-stage-for-more.html?_r=0.

In addition to original podcasts, many radio stations are also recording their live shows and publishing them as podcasts online. This allows fans who miss the live show to listen on their own time. Think of it as DVR for radio. Radio shows that produce podcasts in conjunction with their live broadcasts are more desirable to secure because you reach a wider audience than you would if your interview was only available to those who listen live. It's also easier to share your interview with your social media following because you have a direct link, rather than asking them to tune in at a specific date and time.

Vlogs and Web Series

As podcasts take the place of live radio, video blogs (vlogs) and web series are beginning to take the place of television. This is especially true for the younger generation, who prefer to consume media via their computers, tablets, and phones— some of whom have cut the cord on cable completely.

In essence, vlogs are the same as blogs. The only difference is the format; instead of writing articles, a vlogger will speak their mind on camera. Vlogging is particularly popular in the teen and young adult community (which makes sense based on the age demographic), and many YA authors are having success as vloggers themselves. Additionally, there is a large community called "book tubers" who review books on their own dedicated channels. Again, most of the book tubers are young and focus on YA, but there is also a growing community of romance vloggers. It hasn't caught on within other genre fiction communities or the literary and nonfiction communities yet, but I believe it's only a matter of time.

Vlogs differ from web series, which are structured like television shows but distributed online. Like TV shows, web series come in a variety of formats: news, entertainment, sitcom, drama, etc. As an author, your primary focus will be on news and entertainment shows. Just like you did when looking for appropriate TV shows, you need to find suitable web series that host guests and produce segments.

Finding popular vlogs and web series can take a bit of time, but with YouTube it's easy to see which ones are the most viewed and have the highest ratings. YouTube will also allow you to search similar videos and provide an "If you liked this, you may like this" suggestion with every video you watch. Combing through the various stations takes time, but YouTube is fairly easy to navigate.

While YouTube still reigns as the king of video content, there are other sites like Vimeo and Daily Motion which also host video programs and features. Almost all users post to multiple platforms, so I usually stick to YouTube when it comes to searching for vloggers and web series, but if you find yourself getting stuck, give the other sites a try.

An easy way to understand online media is to remember that for every type of traditional media coverage, there is an online counterpart. Newspapers and magazines equate to websites and blogs. Radio shows equate to podcasts, and television equates to vlogs and web series. And just as with traditional media, the subjects are endless. There are online media outlets for any interest; the only difference is the format. And when it comes to approaching online media contacts, your methods should be similar to those you use for their traditional counterparts.

TIMING

Unlike traditional media, which can require up to seven months of advance notice, online media outlets usually have a far shorter lead time. Much of this depends on how often the outlet publishes new content—most websites and blogs post new content every day, while podcasters and vloggers sometimes only produce 1–2 shows a month. When creating your media list, include notes about how often new content is posted. This will affect how far in advance you need to pitch.

Additionally, while newspapers are tossed in the recycling bin at the end of each day, online content stays around for much longer. Therefore, it's not always necessary for coverage to appear around the time of your book launch. Generating some early publicity can be a great way to build name recognition before the book comes out, as long as it's not so early that people forget who you are by publication date. Ideally, most of your media coverage will release around your pub date, but a few features or interviews a week or two early is still great for generating preorders and early buzz.

People need to hear your name or see your book cover dozens of times before it actually sticks in their brains. If all your coverage hits around launch time, it may be several weeks before people make the leap to buy the book. But if they hear your name and see your book cover image a few times leading up to your publication date, by the time your book comes out and the wave of reviews and interviews rolls in, they'll be poised to buy.

CREATING A MEDIA LIST

Now that you have an understanding of the various online media outlets available to you, you can start creating a media list. Because there are far more online outlets than there are traditional media outlets, your list should be notably longer than your traditional media list, but other than length, the process is fairly similar.

Identify Potential Outlets

To identify which online outlets are the best fit for your campaign, you must first think about your typical reader. When your readers are online, which sites do they view regularly? What newsletters do they subscribe to? What types of content are they interested in reading? Go through the same steps as you did in the "Traditional Media" section.

If you don't spend too much time online and aren't entirely sure of what online media your audience consumes, that's completely okay. Instead of creating your own outreach plan, you can simply borrow someone else's. Identify a book similar to yours, preferably one that came out recently. Plug the book title into google along with keywords like "blog" or "online review" or "podcast" and see what comes up. Compile a list of all the online outlets that covered the book. Chances are, they'd be open to covering yours, too!

Another great characteristic of online outlets is that it's easy to link up or reference similar outlets. Most bloggers feature a blogroll, which is a list of other blogs they read. Vloggers will "favorite" videos from other vloggers, and many podcasts will include links to other shows on their network. Feel free to plunge down the online rabbit hole and see what other opportunities you're able to dig up.

Gauging Traffic

Once you have a solid list of outlets (35–50) you'll need to evaluate whether or not these sites receive any traffic. While many websites and blogs look professional and boast well-written content, you may be surprised by how many of those websites only receive a handful of visitors each month.

The purpose of online media coverage is to expand your name recognition and reach potential readers. Therefore, you should only focus your attention on online outlets with a strong readership.

When evaluating whether or not a site is worth pitching to, I recommend taking a holistic approach. Rather than focusing on one aspect of the data, you should take multiple things into consideration:

Traffic Stats

Sites like SimilarWeb provide a snapshot of how much traffic a website receives. Plugging the URL of a website you're considering into SimilarWeb's data engine will provide the following data:

- Global and country rank – where this website ranks among all websites in the world and the country
- Unique monthly visitors – how many individual people visit the website during a one-month period

- Page views – how many pages those visitors look at before leaving the site
- Bounce rate – how many people come to the site and leave right away
- Average time on site – how long the average person spent on the site

These data points should paint a picture of how much the site is viewed and what users do once they get there. Some sites will have unique visitors in the millions, but if the average time on site is less than a minute or the bounce rate is really high, how many of those people are actually sticking around to read the content? Other sites may have fewer monthly visitors, but a lower bounce rate and higher amount of page views. This means that the people who do visit are actually reading the content. It's always better to have a smaller, engaged audience, as opposed to a larger audience that isn't really connecting.

Social Media Following

Most online outlets have corresponding social media accounts, providing another opportunity to reach readers. Whenever new content is posted to their website or there's a new podcast available, they will post an announcement on Facebook, Twitter, and other social media channels. If the outlet has a large social media following, you'll have an opportunity to reach those followers.

But you should pay attention to more than just the number of followers. For Twitter, you also want to look at the follower-to-following ratio. Many Twitter users will follow people with the sole purpose of receiving a follow-back, boosting their numbers without growing a real audience. For all platforms, you also want to pay attention to the level of engagement. If someone's Facebook page has thousands of "likes," but their individual posts don't receive any likes, comments, or shares, it's a good indicator that those followers aren't actually reading—or even seeing—the content. Keep in mind that users are able to purchase followers to boost their numbers, so just because someone's Facebook page has a high number of likes doesn't mean they have an engaged audience.

Comments and Shares

Not only is this important when it comes to gauging social media engagement, but you should pay attention to these things on the actual website as well. If blog posts are shared frequently, that means more people are seeing the content than just the regular subscribers. Comments are great indicators of engagement. Websites can game the system by using content marketing or SEO tools to drive traffic to their site, but if people aren't actually reading and engaging with the content, what's the point? Remember, the goal is to reach potential readers. If they don't connect with the content, you won't see that conversion.

When evaluating the online outlets on your list, you want to keep all of these aspects in mind. If a site has only a moderate amount of traffic but comments and shares indicate an engaged audience, or the site has a large social media following, then it may be worth your time to contact them. If the traffic is really high but so is the bounce rate and there is limited engagement, then you may want to cross them off your list. Remember, the goal is to reach potential readers. If they don't read and engage with the content, you won't see that conversion.

Finding the Contacts

Once you've culled your media list to only include outlets with a large, engaged audience, you'll use a tactic similar to that discussed in the "Traditional Media" section. Most blogs and websites have clearly displayed contact information; some use contact forms. Occasionally, you'll come across an outlet without any clear contact information. In these instances, it's okay to reach out to the person via Twitter or Facebook message. This shouldn't be your pitch; it should be a short message saying you're trying to get in touch with them about their site and would like their email address. People who write for online outlets tend to be more open to communicating via social media, as long as it's handled professionally.

Like your traditional media list, you'll want to pay attention to which person is the best contact for the content you're pitching. Most bloggers will have a review or PR policy on their site. Read it carefully. For podcasters and vloggers, listen to and view a few shows so you're familiar with what they cover, and try to get in touch with the person most likely to cover your content.

A NOTE ABOUT SEO

While the primary goal of online media coverage is to reach potential readers, there is also a secondary benefit: Search

Engine Optimization, or SEO. If you're a new author, especially one with a more common name, you may notice that Googling yourself won't yield the most desirable results—oftentimes, your website shows up halfway down the page, or even a page or two into a Google search.

Boosting your Google-ability is extremely important when it comes to discoverability; you need to make it as easy as possible for people to find you.

This is where SEO comes into play. There are many companies that will charge you thousands of dollars to boost your SEO, not telling you about the many easy ways you can do it for yourself. One of those ways is securing online media coverage.

When a blogger reviews your book or you write a guest article for a news site, they will include a link to your website. This is called a back-link, and the more back-links you have, the higher your site will show up in Google searches. How much "Google juice" you receive from a back-link will depend on how much traffic that website receives. Securing a back-link on a site like *Huffington Post* or *Salon.com* will give you a bigger boost than a link from a smaller blog.

Because of this, many SEO companies or high traffic websites will attempt to sell you guest post slots. For a fee, you will have the opportunity to write a guest article for a high traffic website and receive a back-link. Google is onto this and will sometimes flag content that is clearly pay-to-play. Avoid the shortcuts and attempt to secure the online media coverage yourself.

Though there are more opportunities for online media coverage than ever before, a large percentage of these outlets don't have a large enough following to make an impact on your book sales. During your research, you may find more than 100 book blogs that would be a good fit for your book, but don't be discouraged if 95 of them only receive a handful of visitors a month. Focus on the quality of the outlets rather than the quantity. This way, you'll be able to reach more readers through less effort.

RESOURCES

SimilarWeb.com
Compete.com
Quantcast.com
Alexa.com

PITCHING

As a publicist, the majority of my time is spent pitching media in an attempt to secure media coverage. This is something that requires a great deal of practice, evaluation of your efforts, and adaptation based on the needs of the media contact.

The most important advice I can offer on the subject of pitching is to remember that on the other end of the email or phone is a person. You would never go up to a person and act like a walking, talking billboard. To make genuine connections, you have to be genuine.

There are many services out there that will blast emails or send press releases on your behalf. There are publicists who send mass emails, assuming that all media contacts are looking for the same information. If you were at a party and there was a person telling the same story or doing the same shtick to everyone he met, you would avoid that person. The key to crafting a successful pitch that will lead to media coverage is to remember that no one person or media outlet is exactly alike and, therefore, each should feel as if your pitch is tailored specifically for them.

THE ASK

This term refers to what you are hoping to gain by pitching to a media professional. Sometimes the ask is for a book review, other times it's for a feature. The ask will vary depending on the outlet and the particular editor you are pitching to. Tailoring your ask for each media contact will greatly increase your chances of securing coverage.

Any successful publicity campaign consists of multiple types of media coverage.

Books Coverage

This is the first type of media coverage people think of when you mention book publicity. It includes book reviews in trade publications, daily newspapers, literary websites, and the books sections of magazines, as well as on-air reviews and interviews on radio stations and TV shows. Since there are millions of books published each year[7] and a declining number of outlets to cover them, books coverage is some of the most competitive and difficult to secure.

Though you may covet that *New York Times* review or a spot on the TODAY show's books round up, statistically

---

7   "Traditional Print Book Production Dipped Slightly in 2013," *Bowker*, last modified August 5, 2014, http://www.bowker.com/news/2014/Traditional-Print-Book-Production-Dipped-Slightly-in-2013.html.

speaking, your chances are slim to none. However, there are a variety of smaller or genre-specific outlets where you'd have a better shot, in addition to your local media outlets and websites and blogs.

Books coverage is the most effective tool in marketing a book because it reaches a captive, targeted audience. People who read the books sections of newspapers or books-centric websites are already interested in learning about new books. The leap from publicity to sales is a lot smaller. So while it may seem that smaller publications and broadcast and online outlets may not have a large reach, there's a strong chance of that small reach translating into sales.

Off-the-Books-Page Coverage

Because books coverage is so competitive, many authors have more success with coverage "off the books page." This refers to features, interviews, and other types of media that don't pertain to books. For example, a review of your middle-grade novel in *Parents* magazine would be considered books coverage, but an article in that same publication about encouraging reluctant readers where you are quoted and your book is mentioned would be considered off-the-books page coverage.

Go back to your branding worksheet and your social media content strategy. Look at the topics that relate to you and your book and think about outlets that may be covering these topics. Some examples of this type of coverage from campaigns we've worked on—which directly tied to themes in the authors' books—include:

- A feature on Yahoo! Parenting about Linda Goodnight, author of *The Memory House*, and her blended family[8]
- A guest article for *Redbook* about starting over after a divorce, written by Sophie Littlefield[9]
- Bill Hillmann's interview with *The Atlantic* about running with the bulls and what it's like to be gored[10]

Rather than pitching a review of these books or an interview discussing the book, we pitched these timely, interesting articles, which all included a mention of the authors' books. These can also be easier to secure because there is less competition for coverage. Not that I'm saying a feature in *Redbook* or on Yahoo! is an easy "get," but there is far more space in the features sections of these publications than there is in the books sections. Online outlets also have far more room to run content than the print publications, so a lot of these pieces will appear online rather than in print.

This type of coverage reaches a broader audience, which has its pros and cons. The benefit of reaching a broader audience is that you may connect with people who aren't dedicated readers, but read on occasion and could be

---

8 Linda Goodnight, "I Was About to Retire Before We Adopted a Teenager," Yahoo! Parenting, February 26, 2015, https://www.yahoo.com/parenting/i-was-about-to-retire-before-we-adopted-a-teenager-111300143477.html.

9 Sophie Littlefield, "I Gave Away Most of My Things After My Divorce—And All My Relationships Improved," *Redbook*, March 31, 2015, http://www.redbookmag.com/home/a21150/after-divorce-i-downsized-from-a-house-to-a-few-small-roomsi-let-go-of-all-my-resentment/.

10 Olga Khazan, "What It's Like to Be Gored at the Running of the Bulls," *The Atlantic*, July 10, 2015, http://www.theatlantic.com/international/archive/2015/07/what-its-like-to-be-gored-at-the-running-of-the-bulls/398126/.

interested in your book if it were presented to them. The cons are that the leap from coverage to sales grows wider because a large percentage of that audience may read the article but don't necessarily read books.

In order to maximize your potential for reaching readers, take a good look at the outlets you're pitching and ask yourself (again) if your target audience consumes this type of media. If the answer is yes, then the coverage is worth it, even if the rate of return is slightly lower.

Guest Articles

As authors, you have an advantage that other people don't: you can write! Print publications are having their budgets cut on a regular basis, and online outlets are being pressured to "feed the beast" by posting multiple articles a day, which means there is a high demand for free content.

There is a lot of controversy about whether or not it's ethical or useful for authors to write for free. I understand the concern; freelance journalists feel they're getting cut out of paying gigs because others are willing to work for free, and since authors get paid to write their novels, why shouldn't they be paid to write content for publications?

I believe that the relationship between media outlets and guest contributors is symbiotic. The author has the opportunity to reach a large audience, earn some Google juice from the back-link, and reinforce their brand. The media outlets are able to save some dough and stay in business, maybe even using those funds to pay other freelancers or keep some of their full-time writers on staff. Freelance journalism is different than writing a few articles in the interest of promotion, and I don't believe one ruins it for the other.

Guest articles can include both books coverage and off-the-books page coverage, depending on where that article appears. Writing about your favorite pulp novels for *Mystery Scene* or about trends in YA for BookRiot is another way to reach that captive audience if a review isn't in the cards. Some outlets also provide the opportunity for an author to write a guest article about some aspect of the book or the author's writing process in addition to a review they run on your book, which offers a way for that audience to see your name and book title more than once. You can also focus your attention on off-the-books page pieces. As a romance writer, you could contribute an article about dating tips or advice for spicing up your sex life to women's publications and websites. A sci-fi author could write about scientific developments predicted by sci-fi authors for tech or science publications.

While a review or feature is more straightforward and has a basic ask, the opportunities for guest articles are more prevalent and can change with the news cycle and developing trends. It's important stay on top of current events, especially when you're in the middle of media outreach. Whether or not you follow prevalent news sources on social media or read a national daily newspaper on a regular basis, stay on top of what's happening in the world and how your brand fits into it.

Using your branding materials, create a list of 5–10 articles that you could contribute to the outlets on your list. Would those articles interest your target readership? Are you more likely to secure a guest article than a book review or feature? If so, then you've found your ask.

Interviews

Like guest articles, interviews can be considered on- or off-the-books page, and they are a great way for potential readers to get to know you. Most readers will say that if they like the author as a person or find he or she interesting, they're more likely to buy their book.

When pitching radio and TV, the ask will usually be for an interview. However, the focus on that interview can change, depending on what the outlet's audience will find the most compelling. For example, a local 10 A.M. talk show may be interested in talking about you and your book with the slant that you're a local author with a new book out, while an early morning drive-time talk radio show will be more interested in the nonfiction topics and themes covered in your book. Do your research and see what the host or producer would be more interested in before crafting the pitch.

Many bloggers and websites will also run interviews with authors. Sometimes these are done by email, other times by online chat, and in some cases via phone or Skype. Each of these options has their pros and cons. Email interviews allow you to control and edit the content, but they're time consuming and don't often feel like an actual back and forth discussion. Online chat is more immediate and feels more like a conversation, but because it's your written words, there's more pressure to craft well-thought-out and well-written responses on the spot. Phone and Skype are the least time consuming and most immediate, but you run the risk of the interviewer taking your responses out of context or not transcribing accurately.

My advice for new writers is, if given a choice, to opt for

an email interview. Once you have experience with the types of questions likely to be asked, have some of your responses down, and feel more confident, you could ask for a chat interview or phone interview, which will save you some time.

Now that you're aware of all the different asks, go through your media list and decide which ask is the best for each contact. As I mentioned in the previous section, you can have multiple contacts for one media outlet, but each of those contacts should be "asked" something different.

THE APPROACH

While many people assume that all media pitching consists of a cold email or phone call, there are actually many different approaches for you to use.

Cold Pitching

Because the brunt of your publicity efforts will happen leading up to your book launch, this is the most common approach you will take. This is a simple, straightforward email or phone call outlining who you are, why you're writing (the ask), and why that ask is timely and appealing to their audience. Most media pros are used to being pitched to, so it doesn't necessarily matter if you've never emailed them before. Remember, media pros are looking for good content just as much as you're looking for media coverage. As long as it's concise, well-written, and demonstrates an understanding of what they cover, then a cold email will never be viewed as a nuisance or spam.

Editorial Calendars

Most magazines and some online outlets use editorial calendars to plan their coverage in advance. These calendars are usually finalized in August and September, and outline themed issues or topics for the coming year. This is primarily used for advertisers, as it allows them to place their ad buys in advance and work out a campaign for the year, but it should also be used for publicity.

Take a look at your list of media outlets and pick out all the monthly/weekly magazines. Go to their websites and see if they have editorial calendars. It's often listed in the "Advertising" section or under "media kit," but occasionally, you'll have to email them for it. Take a look at their upcoming issues and see if any of your pitch topics fall into that category. For example, if you were planning on pitching a dating advice piece, and in February they have a Love issue planned, then pitch the topic for that specific issue. This may mean your feature or guest article will run outside of your planned publicity push, but the chances of securing coverage dramatically increase if it falls in line with something the publication already has planned.

Journalist Newsletters

Just as there are plenty of people seeking media coverage, there are also plenty of journalists and producers looking for interview subjects and experts for pieces they're working on. There are a handful of newsletters that PR pros and experts are able to subscribe to in order to receive those calls for information.

Help a Reporter Out (HARO)

This free newsletter is sent 3 times a day and is the most popular subscription. The upside of this is that these newsletters have the most (and often best) media opportunities. The downside is that there will be a lot of people pitching each one of those opportunities. We have had a lot of success securing media coverage through HARO, so I recommend subscribing but warn you not to get discouraged if many of the emails don't have anything for you or if your first few pitches don't result in coverage. Our team usually only finds 1–2 items to pitch a week, and that's with a client base of 30+. As an individual, you may only see 1–2 opportunities a month that work for you. But that's okay; it's 1–2 more than you'd receive without the newsletter.

Source Bottle

This is similar to HARO in that they send call-outs for media opportunities, but it's a newer service so there are fewer opportunities in each email and the quality of the outlets is a bit lower. However, unlike HARO, Source Bottle has a search feature on their website so that if you miss an email or two, you can search for open opportunities there. They also have a paid feature where they will promote you as an expert to their database of journalists. It's affordable enough that if you're a nonfiction author trying to establish your brand, it may be worth pursuing.

ProfNet

Like the other services, ProfNet emails lead to media opportunities. However, this is a paid service, so the quality of those queries is slightly better and there's less competition from other PR pros and experts. As a PR pro, I have existing media relationships and many producers and reporters reach out to us outside of these newsletter services, so I haven't found these paid subscriptions necessary. But if you have limited time for cold pitching, then the subscription could be worth it.

With all of these newsletters, it's always important to consider the outlet before pitching. There will be many times when you'll see a query that's perfect for you and want to pitch. But as with all media, traditional and online, if it doesn't reach your target audience, a big enough audience, or an engaged audience, then it's not worth your time. Take note of the media outlet the journalist is writing from and go through the same steps you used for creating your media list. If the source is listed as anonymous, they're probably not the best fit.

Source Filing

This tactic is primarily used for nonfiction authors, but if you're a fiction author with timely journalist angles, then this may be worth pursuing. As we outlined in the previous section, many editors, reporters, and producers are actively seeking guests and sources on particular subjects. In these instances, they usually look through their files of past guests or interview subjects, contact PR companies they've worked with in the past, or use journalists' newsletters. Source filing is a proactive way to get on their radar and into their files without sending a specific pitch.

To submit yourself as a source, I recommend creating a

one-sheeter with your bio, background, and a bulleted list of topics you're able to talk about. You can tailor those topics to meet the needs of the outlet. Always include your contact information and links to any previous expert commentary you've provided. Paste that one-sheeter into the body of an email (attachments often lead to emails getting stuck in spam) below a brief introductory email to the media contact. Since it's a more passive or indirect method, you may not see results from these pitches for several months. Therefore, it's often wise to source file well in advance of publication or as the news cycle presents timely opportunities.

User-Generated Content

Many newspapers and websites support user-generated content, allowing people seeking publicity coverage to bypass the whole pitching process. Sites like *Huffington Post* and *BuzzFeed* built a foundation on user-generated content, while local newspapers are turning to it as a way to beef up local coverage without spending more money. Because this content isn't written by staffers or vetted and selected by editors, it doesn't hold the same weight as editorial coverage, but it can be a good back up plan.

Before submitting that content, I recommend reading similar articles written by the staff writers at the publication to get a sense of the tone, style, and type of content that works well for the publication. Also ask yourself if the publication reaches your target audience and provides an opportunity to reach new readers. Lastly, make sure the content you post supports embedded links. You don't want to miss out on Google juice!

PITCHING

With some exceptions, email is the primary tool used to pitch media. Media pros receive hundreds, sometimes thousands of email pitches a day, so it may seem futile to attempt to make your inquiry rise above the din. But if you follow this basic formula for a successful email pitch, you'll increase the chances of your message getting through.

The Formula

A catchy but descriptive subject

The subject line is the first hurdle to clear and determines whether your email is opened or deleted. Something catchy will encourage someone to open the email, but if the subject line is not descriptive of the content you're pitching, then the email will be deleted upon opening. The subject line should also include some indication that you've done your research and this isn't part of a mass email. Some successful subject lines we've used include:

1. Guest Article from Artisan Farmer and Cheese Maker Antonia Murphy
2. 7/21: Latest from Local Author Erica O'Rourke
3. Author and Physician Tackles Ethics in Scientific Advancements

Each of these clearly outlines what the email will include and is tailored to the specific publication (#1 was to a cheese publication, #2 was to a local media outlet, and #3 was to a science/technology website). When your pitch includes something timely like an event or holiday, it's helpful to include the date in subject line as well.

Not sure if your subject line is working? Send a handful of emails using your subject line and see if you get any responses. Even if your contacts write back that they're going to pass, it means they still opened the email and read your pitch, which means your subject line worked. We also use a tool called HubSpot, which tells you when recipients open your email or click on embedded links. It's free for under 200 emails per month and is a great way to gauge the effectiveness of your pitch.

A straightforward, clear, opening paragraph

Within the first paragraph, the recipient should know who you are and why you're writing. More often than not, our team opts for the standard, "I'm with Kaye Publicity and I represent Author X and we're interested in a Y from Z" approach. Within the first line, which usually can be previewed before the email is even opened, they know the ask and have an indication that it's not a mass email or spam. Occasionally, we will use a catchier hook, but we'll get to the who we are part pretty quickly. Two successful openings include:

> 1) I'm writing on behalf of our authors Sophie Littlefield and Denise Grover Swank. These award-winning and bestselling authors will be appearing at Women and Children First on 9/17 and we'd love to book them as guests on Fox News at Noon.

> 2) With the increasingly crowded marketplace and the traditional marketing tactics becoming less

effective, authors and publishers are constantly looking for new ways to generate word of mouth for their titles. And while more and more emphasis is put on digital marketing, there is still no replacement for a personal connection.

Crooked Lane Books author Chris Goff has teamed up with 3 other authors to host a book shower for her upcoming title *Dark Waters*. We'd love this unique marketing idea showcased on *Booklist Online*.

Many authors (and some publicists) are tempted to front-load the pitch with catchy turns of phrase and a long lead-in to the actual point, but in my experience, those are the first emails to get deleted. Stick to the facts and don't waste journalists' time.

A concise outline of what coverage will look like

I've seen too many pitch emails that pose general offers to the recipient, such as, "We'd love to send you a book for your perusal" or "Are you interested in covering the book in your publication?" The easiest way to land the media placement is to do the journalist's or producer's job for them and clearly show them what the coverage will look like and how it will fit into their current editorial mission.

When pitching magazines, it's always great to suggest which section you're looking to secure placement in. If pitching a segment for a morning news show, outline talking points for you to address on air. If you're pitching a guest article, include bullet points outlining the main ideas covered in that article. The easier it is to envision the final piece, the easier it will be to place that piece.

Additional tips for writing a successful pitch email include:

- Never include attachments.
- Embed links in your website, or previous interviews in the body of the email.
- If you're seeking a review, don't include a link to a competitor's review. *USA Today* doesn't care that the *New York Times* already reviewed their book, in fact, they may see it as a jab that you pitched to their competitor first.
- Additionally, when seeking reviews, avoid temptation to fill your pitch with previous reviews of the book. A book blogger may be impressed that you've been reviewed by dozens of daily newspapers, but a critic for a national paper may just think, "If everyone else already reviewed it, why do I have to?"
- If you're pitching a TV or radio appearance, link to any previous interviews that demonstrate your ability to be effective on camera.
- Always use active and direct language. Don't say, "Please contact me if you want additional information." Instead, say, "I'd love to send you additional information and an advance copy of the book."

Timing

Writing the perfect pitch is an art form, but the timing of sending that pitch also takes finesse. Many PR pros will tell you to always pitch Tuesday through Thursday, first thing in the morning. While that's a good general rule of thumb, there's a lot more to it than that.

The first step is to put yourself in the shoes of the person you're pitching to. If you're pitching a show that starts at 6 A.M., chances are that producer is in the studio by 3 A.M. If the show wraps at 9 A.M., they're out of there by 10 A.M. There will have been a swarm of emails from overnight, so first thing in the morning, they're cleaning their inbox, but there will be another wave when the rest of the world gets into the office. And if most PR people are pitching Tuesday through Thursday, pitching on Monday or Friday may yield less competition for that producer's attention. Timing a pitch is more art than science, but keeping records of the days and times that yield the best results will help you determine the optimal time to pitch to your contacts.

On the flip side, most bloggers and website editors have day jobs and may not be able to answer email on weekdays. You may have better luck reaching them in the evening or on the weekends.

The other piece of this puzzle is when *you* are available to send these pitches. You may have a day job, kids, and other obligations that leave you with a very small window to do this outreach. While sending pitches at the prime time for each media outlet will increase your chances for getting placement, pitching at a less-than-optimal time doesn't mean your chances drop to zero. If your time is limited, I recommend drafting emails ahead of time and doing your best to send them at the prime time for each media contact. If you can only send emails at 3 A.M., then it's better than nothing.

In addition to time of day, lead time is also a key factor in pitching media.

As we outlined in the Traditional Media section, the various lead times determine how far in advance we should begin pitching each type of publication. Magazines that publish once a month or less will need a longer lead time, as will book critics who need to read the book. If you're pitching a guest article or blog review, you can usually secure coverage only 4–6 weeks in advance. Every publication is different, and as you build relationships with media contacts, you'll learn their preferred lead times for being contacted.

Once you've sent out an initial pitch via email, it's appropriate to follow-up once via email, usually 7–10 days later. If you still don't have a response after two weeks, and you really believe you and your book would be a great fit for that publication, then it's appropriate to make a phone call.

Some notes regarding phone calls:

- You will usually get a voicemail. Barely any media pros answer their phone anymore. Leave a short voicemail, and if you're nervous about rambling for too long, just read the opening line of your email: "My name is X, I'm the author of Y, and I'm interested in coverage for Z. I sent you an email last week and wanted to make sure it came through. Please give me a call back."
- Speak slowly. Extra slowly. You will be nervous, which means you'll be speaking faster than you usually do.
- Repeat your phone number twice for clarity.

- On the off chance the person you're calling does pick up the phone, you'll want to first make sure you're not catching them at a bad time. There's nothing worse than trying to pitch someone who doesn't have time to be on the phone. In this instance, try something along the lines of, "My name is X and I'm following up about an email I sent last week. Am I catching you at a good time?" If the answer is no, then ask for a better time to reach them. If the answer is yes, then continue your introduction.
- Take pauses and allow them to react to what you're saying. Your inclination will be to just ramble off your entire email until they stop you. If you pause along the way, they may prompt you to continue or ask you for different information than you originally intended to share.
- Always make these phone calls when you suspect people will be in the office. Don't call during the wee hours of the night, just so you don't have to talk to an actual person. Your chances of getting your pitch read after speaking to an actual person are far higher than if you left a voicemail.

Tracking Outreach and Organization

The final piece of the pitching puzzle involves record keeping. Keeping an accurate account of whom you pitched to, when you did, whether or not you followed up, and what their response was is key to building relationships and evaluating the trajectory of your campaign.

Learn Excel. Learn it and love it. It will be your best friend.

Most months, we're managing campaigns for 20–30 books, all at different stages of the pitch process. Most days, we're sending 20–50 pitch emails for a variety of titles. Keeping track of who has responded, who has been followed up with, and who still needs to be contacted requires a detailed system and record keeping. Excel spreadsheets are perfect for that.

I recommend creating tabs based on when you're planning to reach out to those outlets. If your book comes out in September, I recommend creating the following tabs:

- March (this is when you'll pitch to monthly and quarterly magazines)
- April (this is when you'll pitch to additional book critics)
- June (this is when you'll pitch to daily and weekly print publications)
- July (this is when you'll begin pitching to online outlets)

If you're only pitching to a handful of outlets, let's say fewer than 40, you could get away with including all your data on one sheet. Just make sure you make a note of the ideal time to pitch to each outlet.

Populate each tab with the appropriate media contacts from your list. I usually use separate columns for first name, last name, and media outlet. Then add a column for "Date Pitched," "Date Followed Up," and "Notes." The importance of these columns is for sorting. If you only incorporate your actions into the "Notes" section, you aren't easily able to sort the sheets by date and see who has yet to be followed up with. The "Notes" section is where you'll keep a record of when someone responds, requests materials, etc. Update this column as you progress.

On the following pages is a portion of a spreadsheet we used in a recent campaign.

It is clear who has been pitched to, when, and their response. It's also easy to sort based on date to see if there's anyone who hasn't received a follow-up or initial pitch email, or sort by outlet to see if there are any duplicate contacts. The easier it is to categorize and sort your data, the easier it is to ensure nothing gets lost in the shuffle.

As you start pitching on a regular basis, you'll also start building your "rolodex" of media contacts. I find this helpful to track in Excel as well. I include tabs for each type of media contact (magazine, radio, blogger, etc.) with their contact information and any pertinent notes. These can include:

- Coverage you've secured with them
- Recent stories they've covered that are similar to yours
- Feedback re: your pitches (only takes nonfiction, doesn't do reviews, etc.)

Accurate record keeping is essential to pitching effectively and building relationships, and Excel is—for us—a necessary tool for maintaining those records efficiently.

Additional Materials

As you receive responses to your media pitches, you may be asked for additional materials, in addition to an advance copy of your book. It's important to have those materials

First Name	Last Name	Outlet	Date	Follow-up	Notes
Luis	Perez	The Vocalo Morning Amp—WBEW-FM	18-Mar	25-Mar	
Elly	Fishman	Chicago	31-Mar		will feature in June for "One Big Question" segment
Kristi	Turnbaugh	Demo	6-May	19-May	
Jeff	Lyon	*The Columbia Chronicle*, Columbia College Chicago	6-May	19-May	
Aimee	Levitt	*Chicago Reader*	6-May		interested in feature, Irvine Welsh will interview
Brian	Hieggelke	*Newcity*	6-May	19-May	
Scott	Fornek	*Chicago Sun-Times*	6-May	19-May	
Lisa	White	*Chicagoist*	19-May	10-Jun	
Marla	Krause	*The DePaulia*, DePaul University	19-May	10-Jun	
Stacia	Campbell	*The Daily Northwestern*, Northwestern University	19-May	10-Jun	
Tasha	Neumeister	*The Independent*, Northeastern Illinois University	19-May	10-Jun	
Andrew	Huff	*Gapers Block*	19-May	10-Jun	
Brent	DiCrescenzo	*Time Out Chicago*	19-May	10-Jun	
Aurora	Aguilar	The Morning Shift—WBEZ-FM	19-May	10-Jun	
Brian	Dahlen	Karl and June Mornings—WMBI-FM	19-May	10-Jun	
Kate	Gibson	WGN	19-May		wants to book any Saturday now through 6/6

First Name	Last Name	Outlet	Date	Follow-up	Notes
Odette	Yousef	WBEZ	19-May		
Ryan	Morton	The Guy Benson Show—WIND-AM	19-May	10-Jun	
Alan	Thompson	CBS 2 News at 11AM—WBBM-TV	19-May	10-Jun	
Darah	Languido	ABC 7 News This Morning—WLS-TV	19-May		passed; cannot interview on her segment—recommended to pitch Jeff and Emerald-Jane
Emerald-Jane	Hunter	Windy City Live—WLS-TV	19-May		see above
Jeff	Marchese	ABC 7 News This Morning—WLS-TV	19-May		has advised Darah and weekend producer Dan in case they'd like June 6 or June 17 coverage
Jill	Jordan	ABC 7 News This Morning—WLS-TV	19-May		see above
Karen	Konyar	Fox News at Noon	19-May		requested June 3 segment
Katie	McDonough	WGN-TV	19-May		requested segment while in Spain
Marc	Vitali	Chicago Tonight—WTTW-TV	19-May		booked for 6/16
Melissa	Perez	You & Me This Morning—WCIU-TV	19-May	10-Jun	
Kevin	Powell	The Steve Cochran Show—WGN-AM	28-May	10-Jun	
Ken	Smith	The Mancow Morning Show—WLUP	8-Jun		booked for 7am June 18
Adina	Klein	Good Day Chicago—Fox News	25-Jun	30-Jun	

ready so you don't leave your media contact hanging for too long. Those materials could include:

- Links to previous interviews
- Talking points
- Press release/press kit

Most TV and some radio producers will want to get a sense of your personality and make sure you'd do well on their shows prior to booking the appearance. If you've already done media interviews, these should be listed on your website and/or YouTube channel, making it easy to compile. If you haven't participated in broadcast interviews, I recommend creating a vlog or sample interview using a video recorder. It should be less than three minutes long and give viewers a sense of your on-screen persona. Good production quality is a plus, but not necessary. They just want to see you speak comfortably and eloquently on camera.

You will also need to have your talking points clearly outlined and ready to send. Most of these will be created during the branding process, but as you tailor your pitch to different outlets and as relevant events occur in the news cycle, those talking points may shift and change. Create a list of things you are able to discuss as they relate to your brand and your book. How can those things be tailored to interest a TV or radio producer?

For example, one of our authors wrote a YA thriller with a protagonist who had urges to kill. One of her talking points was "Violence in Young Adult literature." While that interested the books and educational outlets, it wasn't universal enough for mainstream media. So, instead, we framed it as, "Violence in Entertainment: How much is too much?" With that talking point, we were able to secure her a handful of radio interviews and a TV appearance.

Talking points are meant to pique a person's interest and give them an idea of what an interview with you would sound or look like. If you only pitch your book, most producers will say they don't cover fiction or they only have limited space for book reviews. But if you include topics above and beyond your book, particularly ones that are timely and newsworthy, they'll envision an interview with you differently.

Media contacts may also request press materials, in the form of a press release or a press kit. A press release is usually 1–2 pages and written in the form of a news story: most important information first, least important last. Before the days of email and media databases, PR pros would send these releases via fax to the newsrooms, and the people working the news desk would field those requests. Now, they're sent over a newswire or via email. Since a new book out doesn't really constitute "news," you won't need to write a press release in the traditional sense. Instead, I recommend a one-sheeter, front and back, that boasts your book cover and includes a synopsis, advance blurbs, concise and professional bio, author photo, talking points, book cover image, and contact information. You can send this one-sheeter via email, but if you're also sending a book, I recommend printing it out and including it in the shipment. That way, if the reviewer loses track of your email or forgets who sent the book, they can reference the press materials.

If you're pitching a review or an interview discussing the book, this one-sheeter will suffice. But if you're pitching a profile or an interview with you, the author, as the focus, then I recommend putting together a press kit.

A press kit is like a highlight reel, an expansion on the one-sheet that encapsulates all aspects of you as an author. It should feature all your books, showcasing the most important titles, as well as a longer bio and more in-depth talking points. It can also include any or all of the following:

- Previous appearances or workshops taught
- Upcoming events/tour dates
- Q&A
- Praise and accolades

I recommend playing up your strengths. If your publisher is sending you on a nationwide tour, it indicates that you have nationwide appeal, which is key for pitching media. If you have dozens of amazing reviews from respected review outlets, then including pull quotes from those reviews will demonstrate your clout. If you have an interesting story behind the idea for this book, it may give producers an idea of how to focus your segment. Identify areas of strength and exploit those in your press kit.

RESOURCES

HelpAReporterOut.com
SourceBottle.com
ProfNet.com
GetSidekick.com

SAMPLE PRESS KIT

Grand Central Publishing
Hachette Book Group
237 Park Avenue, Fl 16
New York, NY 10017

FOREVER

Publicity Contact: Dana Kaye
773-878-0722
Dana@KayePublicity.com

"A love letter to Chicago, the author's true passion."
—*Romantic Times Book Reviews* on *A Black Tie Affair*

"Bodine deftly seasons her sexy contemporary romance with a stylish
combination of captivating characters and a deliciously subtle sense of humor."
—*Chicago Tribune* on *A Black Tie Affair*

"Like a box of the heroine's decadent chocolates -- impossible to resist."
—**Sherryl Woods**, *New York Times* bestselling author on *Talk of the Town*

Sherrill Bodine

An author, world traveler, and
fashionista, Sherrill Bodine's life is
nothing short of fabulous. The Chicago
socialite regularly attends Milan Fashion
week, is a frequent party goer, and is
known for her philanthropy and
fundraising events. She writes about the
high life in her books, published by
Grand Central Publishing, and gives
readers a "behind-the-scenes" look into
Chicago's high society.

Sherrill is frequently featured in *Michigan
Avenue* Magazine, her novel TALK OF
THE TOWN was named a "Red Hot Read"
by Cosmopolitan, and her novel A BLACK TIE AFFAIR was a Fresh
Fiction Fresh Pick.

For contests, fashion tips, or bits of gossip, visit her website:
www.SherrillBodine.com

Books

ALL I WANT IS YOU
January, 2012

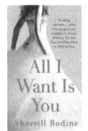

Vintage boutique owner Venus Smith is stunned to realize her newest acquisition comes with a larcenous legend. Stolen years ago, the antique mermaid brooch belongs to the Clayworth family. The right thing to do would be to return it, but that means facing Connor Clayworth O'Flynn, the sexy department store heir Venus has had an unrequited crush on since childhood-and the man who helped ruin her father.

Connor knows that Venus has never forgiven him for what happened between their families. But business isn't personal, even though Venus's father's betrayal still cuts him like a knife. So when Venus proposes a deal-she'll return his family's brooch if he helps clear her father's name-he reluctantly agrees. As action-packed days turn into flirtatious fall nights, it isn't long before old memories resurface . . . and new desires ignite. Can two young lovers leave the past behind? Or must they first admit that all they've ever really wanted . . . is each other?

A BLACK TIE AFFAIR
January, 2010

Fashion curator Athena Smith will do anything to get her perfectly manicured hands on the Clayworth family's celebrated couture collection for her exhibit. So when she's called in to make sure the gowns are the real deal, she's ecstatic...until a dress she's examining turns out to be loaded with toxins (talk about killer threads!) and Athena faints dead away, only to wake up face-to-face with the One That Got Away, notorious Chicago banker Drew Clayworth.

Drew still believes Athena betrayed him all those years ago, and he's sure he can't trust her. But when the priceless gowns go missing, she offers to help track them down. Reluctantly allied in the quest, Drew and Athena are soon stunned by the barely restrained passion still sizzling between them...and memories both bitter and sweet.

"A witty and sexy new contemporary romance" —RomanceJunkies.com

"An engaging, romantic story, be sure to look for A BLACK TIE AFFAIR" —Romance Reviews Today

"This book isn't just another story about a shallow fashionista looking for her rich and handsome forever love. *A Black Tie Affair* has substance with themes such as family loyalty verses loyalty to self, fighting for what you believe in, and looking beneath the surface—not just in people but in situations." —Feminist Review

TALK OF THE TOWN
December, 2009

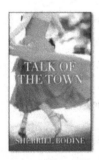

What a to-do at the Daily Mail today! After fifteen years as Chicago's gossip guru, Rebecca Covington has been demoted from divulger of secrets for the city's elite to headlining recipes in the Home and Food section. Apparently, a touchy senator is threatening legal action for Rebecca's latest extramarital scoop. But Windy City rumor has it that new CEO and dreamy Pierce Brosnan–look-alike David Sumner downgraded Rebecca in favor of fresher, younger blood on the social beat.

Industry insiders expect Rebecca to fight her denouement, and inquiring minds have already seen the feisty maven trading quips and searing glances with her arresting new boss. Rebecca swears she'll reclaim her shining star status, but the dishy diva's new boss must be wondering if Rebecca can even cook. Meanwhile, how can Rebecca ignore David's arousing effect on her sensibilities?

"Sherrill Bodine provides a warm, amusing gender war between the spunky reporter and her reticent boss." —Harriett Klausner

"Fun and sassy" —Romance Reviews Today

"Full of juicy gossip, captivating romance and scrumptious recipes that are sure to spice up anyone's life!" —Fresh Fiction

About the Author

Family
Born in Lafayette, Indiana, Sherrill grew up in her grandmother's house, taking care of her mentally disabled mother. Though difficult at times, the experience forged her philosophy that, "We're all in this together – and we need to embrace each other with as much grace, humor, and compassion as we can muster."

She eloped with her husband at the age of eighteen and they went on to have four children. Despite being married more years than Sherrill cares to admit, she claims he is still her prince charming.

"I'm a complete fashion addict and world traveler."
—*Sherrill*

Writing
Sherrill has been writing stories since junior high, when she won a pair of silver skates in a state-wide essay contest. While her children were young, she sold stories to *Fate Magazine*, *Home Life Magazine* and *True Confessions*. In 1988, she sold my first novel and a week later received a two-book contract from Fawcett. Sixteen novels later, she continues to receive awards, rave reviews, and is never short of material.

Film and Fashion
Sherrill's passion for film was born at the age of five. Her mother loved going to the movie theatres and it became Sherrill's job to take her every weekend. Often they would see four movies in one day.

The fabulous clothes designed by legendary Hollywood icons fueled her interest in vintage and current fashion. Sherrill says her interest in fashion is an ongoing "continuing education" as she regularly attends runway shows for new and established designers. This past fall she attended Milan Fashion Week and was in the audience at the Versace and Gucci Runway Shows and the Bally Presentation.

Travel
Sherrill's thirst for travel has taken her around the world several times. She has gone on safaris in Africa, cruises on the Nile, a journey around Cape Horn, and attended the Olympic Games in China. This year, she attended a wedding in Transylvania and celebrated the Chinese New Year in Hong Kong. Sherrill is a contributor to Jet Set Extra, where she writes about all her fabulous adventures.

A Conversation with Sherrill

What inspired you to finally write under you own name?

My agent, Danielle Egan-Miller. I felt it was time to reinvent myself and she suggested I become myself! I'm active on several charity boards in the city so often I'm photographed at social events. Sometimes those pictures make it into newspapers and magazines - it's nice to be identified as "Author, Sherrill Bodine". I was amazed to discover how many people didn't know I was a writer. Now they do!

How much of your books are based on actual people and places?

It's true, I do write about actual people - but personalities and body parts are mixed and matched - and I always change the names to protect the guilty - the innocent don't need protecting. Chicago is such a great city full of wonderful, caring people. I want to share all of it with the readers - give them a peek behind the scenes and a glimpse beneath the glitter to Chicago's heart.

How have your travels influenced your writing?

Travel is one of my passions - the sights, the sounds, the smells. I love it all! I especially love the people I've met - discovering the common ground I share with women all over the world. My dream is to write about my travels - share my adventures with readers. Now if only I could find an editor who is interested - my bags are packed!

What do you enjoy about being an author?

The readers. I love hearing from them. I read all the reviews they post for my books - the good and the bad - OK, I confess, some of the bad ones have driven me to soak in a hot bath while sipping either tea or champagne - this ritual is my panacea for all stress.

Anything you dislike?

Waiting for the editor to love or hate - reject or accept - the world and characters I've put all my blood, sweat and tears into creating.

What books do you enjoy reading?

I read fiction written by my friends, biographies, books on fashion and travel, and since I'm always trying to improve my storytelling skills, I read books on writing.

What advice can you offer aspiring writers?

I have two signs on my desk. One reads: Most of the important things in the world have been accomplished by people who have kept on trying when there seemed to be no hope at all. The other reads: just when the caterpillar thought the world was over, it became a butterfly. I think they pretty much say it all!

* * * *

Sherrill would love to drop in to your book club, visit your library, or speak at your event. Please direct all booking inquiries to:

Dana Kaye – Kaye Publicity
(773) 878-0722
Dana@KayePublicity.com

SOCIAL MEDIA

INTRODUCTION

Social media continues to be the bane of most authors' existence. They view it as time consuming, confusing, and something they *have* to do. The huge amount of misinformation on how to market yourself on social media doesn't help the cause; articles saying you *have* to be on certain platforms or services offering to triple your following for one low price. I completely understand why authors cringe at the mere mention of social media presence.

This section isn't meant to sell you on social media. It's meant to outline all the different platforms, help you determine which ones are best for reaching your target audience, and demonstrate how to use them in efficient and productive ways. In my experience, once people identify the platform that speaks to them and they learn how to use it properly, it doesn't seem like a chore.

PURPOSE

I don't believe social media sells books. People are usually shocked when I tell them this, but it's true. The purpose of social media is not to directly sell books; it's much more than that.

Brand Building

Maintaining an active social media presence is the easiest way to establish your author brand. You do this through the type of content you post, the users you engage with, and the people you're connected to.

Reader Engagement

Most full time novelists write one book a year, sometimes two. There will be publicity and marketing around each book launch, but in between books your readers won't be seeing your name on every website, newspaper, or TV show. Through social media you're able to engage with your readers in between books and keep your name out there after the main promotional blitz is complete.

SEO and Discoverability

The more content you put out there and more back-links you have, the better chances you have at driving new traffic to your website and other online platforms. By having an active social media presence, you increase the likelihood of new readers or industry pros stumbling across your content.

Book sales are tangential benefits of social media, but, as stated previously, they're not the primary goal. You may be thinking, "Great! That means I can skip this section and forget about social media!" and you're partially right. Because social media does not directly result in sales, then, in theory, you can move on to the next section. However, if it helps your career in other ways, and can tangentially lead to sales, then why wouldn't you give it a shot? Unlike publicity, which you have limited control over, social media is a free marketing tool that provides complete control. If you want to do everything you can to successfully promote your book, then read on.

PLATFORMS

Twitter

In many ways, Twitter is the simplest of all the social media platforms, and yet, it's the one most authors have difficulty with. The concept is straightforward: you share posts of 140 characters or less with your followers. Whenever someone you follow posts something, it will show up in your feed. That's it. While the basics of using Twitter are extremely simple, utilizing it is where people start to get confused.

The Lingo

FOLLOWERS: These are people who have opted to follow your tweets. When you post an update, your content will show up in their Home feed.

FOLLOWING: These are people you've opted in to follow. Their updates will appear in your Home feed. Keep in mind that all content is searchable; you can find tweets about certain people or subjects even if you don't follow them.

@ REPLIES: Your Twitter handle includes an @ at the beginning, so when you're speaking directly to someone on Twitter, you should always use their full handle (@Dana_ Kaye, @KayePublicity, etc.). When someone you follow posts something you'd like to respond to, you can hit the reply button and their handle will automatically come up in the compose field. They will be alerted of your reply, and users who follow both of you will see your conversation.

In addition to @ replies, handles are also used to tag users in a conversation. For example, rather than tweeting, "I'm reading YOUR BOOK, YOUR BRAND by Dana Kaye," you should tweet "I'm reading YOUR BOOK, YOUR BRAND by @Dana_Kaye." This will alert me that someone mentioned me in a tweet; plus, it serves as a plug for that person or brand. If you're not using people's Twitter handles regularly in tweets, you're not using the platform to its full potential.

RE-TWEETS (RTS): When someone posts content that you'd like to share with your followers, you are able to re-tweet or RT their content. Hitting the RT button (the two arrows at the bottom of the tweet) will simply re-post the tweet, or you can add your own content by opting to "quote tweet." When a post appears in your feed with an RT, you know that the content following came from someone else.

LIKE (♥): If you like someone's tweet and want to give them a nod, but don't need to share that tweet with your followers, you should opt to favorite that tweet by clicking on the heart at the bottom of the post. It's a great way to network with other users and let them know you enjoy their content without clogging your feed with RTs.

HASHTAGS: These tags serve as labels for ongoing discussions. They're sometimes used for live events (#Election2016, #SuperBowlXXII) or ongoing discussion topics (#FridayReads, #AmWriting). The purpose of these labels is to connect with other users posting about the same topic and increase your discoverability. Posting about the Super Bowl is timely, but only the people who follow you will see it. If you use the official hashtag, it will make your post visible to anyone who follows or searches that tag.

To identify trending hashtags, I recommend using hashtags.org. This site tracks the top trending hashtags and can also provide you with analytics on any hashtag you input. If you see someone using a hashtag like #WriterWednesday, you can plug it in to hashtags.org and it will generate a report showing when the tag is used, the top users posting the tag, and a sampling of recent tweets. Not only are you able to identify whether or not a hashtag is worth implementing, but it will also give you a snapshot of the types of people using the tag.

Hashtags can be especially useful when attending a conference, trade show, or other large scale event. There is often an official hashtag for the event so that attendees are consistent in their social media posts and can connect with other people at the event. Posting pieces of advice heard at panels or photos from the event, along with the official hashtag, will increase your discoverability and allow you to reach other people at the event.

While this is the official use of hashtags, the language of Twitter has also evolved and is using hashtags to convey a sort of Twitter footnote. You may have noticed tweets like these:

"I've eaten two donuts before 9am
#sorrynotsorry"

"Windows 10 has crashed for the hundredth
time today #headdesk"

These hashtags are not official and don't increase your discoverability in any way. Just because these footnote hashtags are a part of the Twitter language doesn't mean you have to use them.

Audience

This platform is mostly used by the movers-and-shakers within an industry. In publishing, most agents, editors, publicists, and media pros report they prefer Twitter to other social media platforms. Many librarians and booksellers also utilize this platform more than others. The typical Twitter user also skews slightly younger.

Facebook

This is the most widely used social media platform, but it can also be the toughest to game. It seems like everyone, from college students to your eighty-year-old aunt, has a

Facebook account. Based on users, utilizing Facebook will reach the widest possible audience, but because of how the site displays content, those users can be difficult to reach.

The Lingo

FRIENDS: Facebook users you're connected to through your Facebook profile who can see your content.

LIKES: Liking is how users connect with Facebook pages. By liking a Facebook page, you will start seeing their content show up in your feed. Liking can also reference a post; you can like someone's Facebook post as a way to interact with their content without writing a full comment.

Facebook recently incorporated additional "reactions." Now, users can respond with a "Love," a frowny face, etc. This allows users to have more dynamic reactions to content instead of a generic "like." If it feels natural to utilize these reactions, go for it, but from a social networking and branding standpoint, the classic "Like" button works just fine.

COMMENT: Like a blog, users can post comments about the content in their feed. Commenting on other users' posts is a great way to increase discoverability, as your name will be visible to all your friends' friends.

SHARE: Re-posting someone else's content on your profile, a friend's profile, or your author page.

How Content Is Displayed

Unlike Twitter, which displays content solely based on when

the people you follow tweet, Facebook uses an algorithm to display content it thinks you want to see based on your previous interactions. For example, if your friends post photos of their dogs or articles about amazing animals, and you like or comment on that type of content, Facebook is going to label you as an animal lover and show you more of that content. If other friends post links to political articles or polls, but you never like or comment on them, then Facebook won't show you that type of content.

This also applies to the people you interact with on Facebook. If you comment on and like content from certain people more than others, then those people's content will show up in your feed more often.

Additionally, the more people like, comment, share, or click on a single post, the more likely it is to show up in users' feeds. You can have a friend that you never interact with post something you would never click on, but if hundreds of your friends are clicking and commenting on it, that post will show up in your feed.

This factor is the most important, because it is the only one you have some control over. By posting content that encourages readers to engage, you increase the likelihood of users seeing your content.

If you're posting extremely important content (the launch of your next book, an upcoming event) and you want to ensure your followers see your post, Facebook also offers the opportunity for pages to "boost" a post which guarantees that your followers (and their friends, depending on which audience you decide to target) see your content. You can identify boosted content because there's a tiny "sponsored" sign in the corner of the post. The cost varies depending on how many people are following you, but it's usually a very affordable way to push your content out there.

Posting

Unlike Twitter, Facebook does not have a character limit on posting, and, therefore, Facebook posts tend to run a bit longer. Hashtags are supported, but not as commonly used. You're also able to tag people in posts, but instead of using their handle, you simply start typing their name with an @ in front of it and Facebook will automatically display suggestions for whom to tag. It sometimes takes a second, and you may have to type out the entire name before Facebook suggests the correct person. You're also able to include a location for your posts, which can be helpful if you're at a bookstore, conference, or another location that reinforces your brand.

Profile vs. Pages

There is much debate over which type of Facebook platform should be used by authors—a profile, a page, or both. When Facebook first launched, it was only open to college students and there were only profiles. Then, when Facebook opened up to the general public, they rolled out pages for businesses, celebrities, and organizations to use. Both types of platforms have their advantages and disadvantages, and as Facebook continues to change their algorithms, the best platform for authors continues to change.

A personal profile is what most Facebook users have. It allows you to connect with people by "friending" them and liking, commenting on, and sharing their content. You can have a maximum of 5,000 friends, after which people can follow your content but aren't actually friends with you. Most authors would rather have a personal profile because it's more versatile and allows them to interact with their readers more easily. However, a personal profile can be somewhat limiting as a marketing tool.

A Facebook page, as mentioned previously, is used by businesses, celebrities, and large organizations. This works best for authors who plan to utilize their page for marketing and will quickly exceed the 5,000 friend cap. As a person, a Facebook page is limiting because you're only able to like, comment, and share the content of other pages, not profiles. It's also harder to connect with people. You can invite people to like your page, but most people are hesitant, as they know pages are primarily used for promotional tools. Sending a friend request feels more personal, while liking a page is more of a one-way street. These factors deter most authors from focusing on Facebook pages.

However, Facebook pages are far more powerful marketing tools than profiles. With a page, you're able to boost your content, run Facebook ads, and promote upcoming events. With a page, you're also able to see the stats on how many people saw your post, the demographics of your following (how old your followers are, where they live, etc.), and your estimated reach. None of this data is available for a personal profile.

There are clear pros and cons to each platform, and ultimately, you have to go with your gut. If you're a first-time author, you may want to start with a Facebook profile and convert it to a page once you garner a decent following. If you're a veteran author or a debut who signed a major deal, you may want to hit the ground running with an author page so you can utilize all the marketing tools.

Facebook does allow you to convert your profile to a page if it meets certain criteria. Plugging the terms "Facebook convert profile to page" into Google will yield step-by-step instructions on how to do this.

Audience

As mentioned in the introduction, Facebook is the most widely used social media platform and has users from all ages, locations, and professions. However, while younger people have Facebook accounts, they don't use them as much as they used to. (Probably because their parents, grandparents, and teachers all have profiles too.) Facebook is the best way to target general consumers, especially those over the age of 40.

Tumblr

First launched in 2007, Tumblr is a micro-blog platform. Unlike WordPress and TypePad, which support long-form blog posts, Tumblr allows users to just post images, videos, and links to their blog. Like Twitter, Tumblr utilizes a feed; whoever you follow will show up in your feed purely based on when you post. There is no algorithm.

Tumblr is a highly visual platform, and most Tumblr users interact with content from their feed. However, because it is also a blog, people can access your Tumblr page without actually following you. For example, you can see our content at www.KayePublicity.tumblr.com without following us on

Tumblr or even having a Tumblr account. But if you don't follow us, our content won't show up in your feed.

The Lingo

THEME: Like other blogging platforms, Tumblr supports different blog themes. These are templates that will determine your blog's layout, color scheme, etc.

FOLLOW: If you visit a Tumblr blog's URL, you'll see a button in the corner that says "Follow+." By clicking this you will follow the blog, and its content will appear in your home feed. Like Twitter and Facebook, having someone follow you means your content will show up in their feed.

RE-BLOG: Re-blogging is similar to an RT on Twitter or a "Share" on Facebook; you are taking someone's post and re-posting it to your blog. This is a great networking tool, since your name will appear on the original post list as someone who re-blogged, which will signal to the creator that you liked their content. Re-blogging is very common practice on Tumblr; many blogs you'll see consist almost entirely of re-blogged content. However, as an author, you should be sure to post plenty of original content and not rely on just re-blogging other posts.

HEART: Similar to "Likes," a heart indicates you enjoyed the post without sharing it on your own blog. This should be done when you like the content someone posted, but don't think it works for your brand or wouldn't be relevant to followers of your own blog.

Hashtags: On Tumblr, hashtags work a bit differently than they do on Twitter. On Twitter, you don't need to label every keyword or search term with a hashtag, because the text itself will show up in searches. But since Tumblr content is almost always visual, those keywords won't appear unless you add them. If you don't add hashtags to a photo or graphic post, then there's no way users can stumble upon your post during a search. For example, if you post an image of your book cover, you'll want to add the title of your book, your author name, the genre, and the word "book" to the hashtag field.

To determine the best hashtags for your content, I recommend typing a variety of book-related hashtags into the search field and seeing which ones are being used most often. Also take note of the content those tags are referencing and what other tags people are using to identify their work.

One final note about hashtags; you want to ensure that the tag you're using accurately labels your content. I've seen many users try to game the system by applying highly searchable keywords in an attempt to lure people in. But if the content doesn't interest those who would be searching for those terms, then you're not building an audience. For example, using the tag #OneDirection to attract teens and tweens to your YA novel is a smart move, but if the content has nothing to do with One Direction, then those teens and tweens aren't going to click further. When choosing your hashtags, I recommend asking yourself, "If someone searched this term, and then found my content, would it be what they were looking for?"

Posting

As noted in the introduction, Tumblr is a highly visual platform. Whenever you post content to Tumblr, it's important to incorporate a visual component. When posting a link to an article, Tumblr will usually generate a link preview with an image, similar to Facebook. If it doesn't, then you'll want to add your own. If you're posting an inspirational quote, incorporate that quote into a graphic using Photoshop, Canva, or PowerPoint to give it a visual element.

Here are some examples:

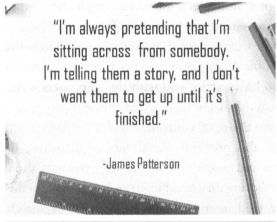

You can post the image by itself (with the appropriate hashtags of course) or add a few lines of content.

Tumblr also supports videos and text content, but the most effective content is images and links.

Instagram

This is one of the most rapidly growing social media platforms, especially among teens and twenty-somethings. Instagram is a photo sharing platform, allowing users to take phòtos and videos, add photography filters and effects, and then share them with their followers. There is also a function to cross-post those images to Twitter, Facebook, and Tumblr. Instagram's popularity grew because everyone wants to be an artist, and with this app, users were able to transform their camera phone images into works of art (and then share them, of course).

Like the previous social media platforms, there are followers and people you're following, you have the ability to like (by clicking on a heart icon) and comment on the photos in your feed, and hashtags are utilized as search terms. Facebook purchased Instagram in 2012, and since then the two platforms have been highly integrated. Instagram will notify you when one of your Facebook friends downloads the app, and you're able to find Instagram users based on your Facebook friends. In fact, most of your Instagram followers will first find you through Facebook.

While it's a popular platform, it can be a bit more difficult than Facebook or Twitter to generate a following, and most of the people who follow you on Instagram probably already follow you on other social media channels. You can increase your discoverability by utilizing hashtags, but, for the most part, people aren't finding people through keywords or a friend's recommendation.

The primary purpose of having an Instagram presence isn't to generate a new following, but to increase interaction with the following you already have. It's a way to engage with your existing readership in between books and stay fresh in their minds. Though there are many authors who have a strong Instagram following, it's usually because they already built a following somewhere else.

However, there are exceptions to the rule, and these users are referred to as Instagram influencers. They have built large followings and use their feeds to spread the word about various products. An example of an Instagram influencer is @CaliforniaDreams. Her feed is a mix of products she sells on her site, as well as books she's reading, food she's eating, and fashion she's excited about. Most of the products featured were sent to her by the manufacturers, in hope that she'd feature those products on her feed. Whether it's a pair of Chanel slippers or the latest YA novel, with her large, interactive following, she has the power to move product.

If your target audience consists of teens and young adults, then it's important to have an Instagram account. But don't get discouraged if your following comes in a slow trickle rather than a wave. And while it's important to update regularly, just so your profile doesn't go stale, your primary focus should be on identifying influencers and reaching out to send them a copy of your book.

LinkedIn

Unlike other social media sites that support more general content, LinkedIn's mission is to connect business professionals for the purposes of networking and advancing their careers. Though I haven't found it to be a useful tool for fiction authors, it is a crucial part of successfully marketing most nonfiction. It can also be a useful tool for authors looking for work in the professional sector (teaching positions, journalism opportunities, etc.).

Your LinkedIn profile reads like a résumé, boasting employers, volunteer work, and skills. The tone is straightforward and professional, unlike the cutesy and witty tone of other social media platforms.

The Lingo

CONNECTIONS: Similar to Facebook friends, on LinkedIn you "connect" with users you know, and those people are able to accept or reject those requests. You can also view second and third degree connections, users to whom you are connected by a mutual friend or a friend of a friend. Only those who are first-degree connections will see your updates, and only those who are second- or third-degree connections will come across your LinkedIn profile in a Google search.

ENDORSEMENTS: Your profile contains a list of skills, and your LinkedIn connections are able to endorse specific skills by clicking on the ones they know you're good at. You can also endorse specific skills they possess by clicking on each one you've seen them display. It's a nice way to help out your fellow connections and build relationships. When people endorse your skills, it doesn't necessarily help sell more books, but it does add to your overall credibility.

RECOMMENDATIONS: These serve as references for your

online résumé. Your connections are able to write about their experience working with you. Again, these don't really translate into sales, but if you write nonfiction and are interested in leveraging speaking engagements or guest appearances on TV and radio, these recommendations add to your credibility.

Posting

As with the rest of the site, the content posted on LinkedIn tends to be more professional, straightforward, and industry related. Links to articles work really well, as do general tips and advice. Unlike other platforms, there doesn't need to be a visual element associated with the content.

In addition to posting updates, LinkedIn also encourages networking with your connections. You'll see prompts to endorse your connections' skills or offer them congrats on their work anniversary.

The feed on your homepage consists of more than just your connections' updates. You'll also see when people make new connections and comment on articles and other activity around the site.

YouTube

As young people cut the cable cord, more and more users are flocking to YouTube as a source for video content. Web series and video blogs (vlogs) are growing in popularity, which is something many authors can take advantage of. If you are a little more tech savvy and, as we say in the industry, "media-genic" (attractive, charming, and comfortable on camera), then building an audience on YouTube is something you may want to consider.

Keep in mind that vlogs and video content take time, and often money, to produce. Consider the investment it would take to execute well and whether or not you would earn the return on that investment.

Around 2007, we started to see a surge in book trailers, mini-commercials for books in the vein of movie trailers. They were all the rage and considered to be the next big thing. However, most of them didn't work. And yet, there are still plenty of authors and companies producing these expensive, mediocre book trailers, throwing them up on YouTube, and expecting to generate a buzz for the book.

There are two reasons why book trailers don't usually lead to sales. The first is that book people don't need to watch a commercial to get interested in a book; that's not how we consume our information or learn about new things to read. Watching a video of an author talk about their book, maybe, but a straightforward ad or movie-type preview won't get us to download or run out and buy a book. It's a different medium.

The second reason is the lack of distribution. Just because you made a trailer and put it up on YouTube doesn't mean people are going to view it. Without a way to distribute that content, you're not going to reach new readers. You can purchase YouTube advertising, which will put your video at the top of searches and feature it in the sidebar while people watch similar movies, but since we're so immune to advertising, those videos are often overlooked. You can team up with other vloggers and bloggers to share the trailer, but if you're going to ask them for something, wouldn't you rather have them review your book?

I'll touch on an exception to the book trailer rule in the "Additional Marketing" section, but 99 times out of 100, a book trailer is something worth skipping.

The Lingo

CHANNEL: Your YouTube channel is like a homepage of your website. This is where the videos you upload will be displayed, as well as videos you add to your channel from other people's pages. You are able to add multiple channels to one account, which is something I recommend doing if you're planning on using YouTube as your primary social media platform.

SUBSCRIBERS: By subscribing to a channel, you will receive notifications whenever new content is added to that channel. The more subscribers you have, the more people will be alerted.

Posting

It's fairly easy to post video content to YouTube; simply click "Upload" and follow the on-screen instructions. The key points to remember are:

- Use a catchy but descriptive title.
- Utilize tags and keywords to attract the target audience.
- Unless it's a training video or webinar, keep all videos under 3 minutes.

We'll address content in greater detail in the following section.

Pinterest

Remember when you'd tear out a recipe or craft project from a magazine and tack it to a corkboard? Pinterest brings that concept online and allows users to take articles from around the web and pin them to their online boards. This platform is mostly used by women and, like Facebook, spans a wide range of ages. It's frequently used by young women getting married to pin wedding dresses or floral arrangements, but it's also used by older women to pin craft patterns and recipes. If your target audience is women and your book is female-centric, then Pinterest is a good place to focus your time.

The Lingo

PINNING/PINNED/PIN IT: A pin references the online corkboard metaphor; when you pin an article, it's like you're tearing it out of a magazine and fastening it to your personal corkboard. Clicking the "pin it" button will take an article and save it to your board.

BOARDS: In real life, having dozens of different boards for different projects would classify you as a hoarder, but with Pinterest, you can create as many boards as you want. Boards allow you to organize your pins into different categories like "Crafts" and "Recipes." Board titles should be simple and descriptive rather than clever.

FOLLOWERS/FOLLOWING: Like all the social media platforms before it, Pinterest allows you to follow people's updates. You're able to follow users, which would allow you to see everything they pin, or to choose specific boards. If you like the majority of what a user is pinning, then you should follow the user, but if you're only interested in one of their boards, you're able to follow that particular board.

RE-PIN: Similar to re-blogging or re-tweeting, re-pinning takes someone else's pin and pins it to your own board. Re-pinning is not only a great way to populate your boards, but it also helps to network with other Pinterest users and build your following.

Posting

Pinterest makes it really easy to pin content from around the web. You can do it manually, by clicking on one of your boards, then clicking "add pin" and following the on-screen instructions. Most internet browsers also support a Pinterest integration which adds a "Pin It" button to your bookmarks bar. When you come across a recipe or project that you want to pin, you can click the button and add it to your boards without visiting the Pinterest site.

Keep in mind that the goal of using any social media platform is to build an audience. Therefore, rather than always pinning content from around the web, you also want to pin links that lead to your website. For example, if you write cozy mysteries that include a craft, consider posting one of those crafts on your blog and then pinning your blog post to a board. If you write business books and have infographics to share, you should post those infographics to your website, then pin a link that leads there. Maintain a balance between pins with links to your website and links to elsewhere on the web; you don't want to come across as overly promotional. We'll address this further in the next section.

Reddit

This link aggregation platform is one of the most overlooked social media marketing tools. Reddit has millions of users, most of whom use the platform on a regular basis. The majority of their users are men, ages 18–24[11], and these users are more tech savvy than most.

One aspect of Reddit that's both a blessing and a curse is that it's a very close and supportive community that's skeptical of outsiders attempting to market to them. People who are active Redditors have had a lot of success reaching new readers on this platform, but outsiders who come in and try to promote their content are quickly shunned.

Before you start promoting your work on Reddit, I recommend taking a few months to engage and become an active part of the community, and we'll discuss ways to do so below. You'll have better luck reaching readers.

The Lingo

REDDITOR: An active Reddit user

SUBREDDIT: The platform is divided up into different content categories called subreddits. These include general topics such as books and politics, as well as more specific niches like "cringe pics" and "anime suggest."

---

11 Ingrid Lunden, "Pew: Reddit Used by 6% of U.S. Online Adults, Putting It on Par with Tumblr, But Far Behind Facebook," TechCrunch, July 3, 2013, http://techcrunch.com/2013/07/03/pew-reddit-used-by-6-of-u-s-online-adults-putting-it-on-par-with-tumblr-but-far-behind-facebook/.

Up Vote/Down Vote: Voting content up or down is the foundation of Reddit. Users will post links to articles or general text posts, and the Reddit community can vote that content up or down, using the arrows to the left of the headline. If the content is interesting and you want more people to see it, you vote up. If it's offensive, too self-promotional, or not appropriate for that particular subreddit, you vote down.

The more up-votes a link has, the higher it will appear on the subreddit home page. The content with the most up votes appears on Reddit's front page.

Link Karma/Comment Karma: When you post new links or comment on other users' content, you will earn one point of karma. This indicates to other Reddit users how active you are in the community. If all you do is post links and never leave comments, your lack of karma points will indicate to people that you're not engaged in the community.

AMA: This stands for "Ask Me Anything" and is a subreddit with a live, interactive component where a person will introduce themselves and the community is able to ask them anything for a certain period of time, say, from 7–8 P.M. on a Tuesday. Questions are posted in the form of comments, and the person replies to as many as they'd like. AMAs have been done by celebrities and politicians, but also regular people who have insights to share. These are usually announced ahead of time so that interested community members can make it a point to join in.

If you are active on Reddit and your work is geared towards Reddit's demographic, then running an AMA the week of your book launch is a great way to generate buzz.

Posting

To submit a new link or text post to Reddit, simply click the "Submit a new link" or "Submit a new text post" buttons in the upper right corner and follow the on-screen instructions. Like YouTube, you'll want to use a catchy but descriptive title. It's also important to submit your content to the appropriate subreddit. If you have an article about the best graphic novels of 2016, it can go into "books," "book suggestions," or "book lists." Sometimes the more specific subreddits are more effective for reaching an audience.

As mentioned previously, in order to become recognized as an active member of the community, I also recommend voting articles up or down, and commenting on a regular basis. This will ensure that by the time you post something more promotional, people won't see you as someone who is just trying to sell them something.

Google+

I save this platform for last because it is something everybody needs, and yet, no one really needs. Let me explain.

When Twitter and Facebook exploded on the scene and the number of social media users grew exponentially, Google wanted to get in the game. They have the most popular search engine, email, and online calendar, so why shouldn't they strive to build the most popular social media platform?

After a few failed attempts (Google Buzz, Google Friend Connect), they officially rolled out Google+ in 2011. It was a strange combination of Facebook and Twitter. You added people to "circles" instead of becoming their friends, there wasn't a real feed, and it was overall confusing. When people are confused about a platform, they don't use it. And it hasn't gotten any better since 2011.

The problem is, while they have a failed social media platform, they also have the most powerful search engine in the world. So they're able to incentivize people and businesses to use Google+ in exchange for giving them a bigger push in the searches.

There was a study done a couple years ago[12] which indicated that when people connected with a site on Google+ or shared a site on their Google+ stream, that website received a boost in Google searches. Therefore, Google+ is less about social networking and more about search engine marketing.

When it comes to Google+, I believe it's important to have an account that is up to date and aligned to your website. That is a must. If you have the time and are able to cross post some of your content from Twitter and Facebook, even better. But since the platform doesn't actually help expend your name recognition and build your brand through content or connecting with actual people, your time is better spent elsewhere.

The Best Platforms for You

Seeing all the different social media platforms, their unique rules, and the different ways they are used can seem overwhelming. Truthfully, trying to maintain a strong presence on every one of these platforms *is* overwhelming.

---

12 Matthew Peters, "2013 Search Engine Ranking Factors," *MOZ*, July 9, 2013, https://moz.com/blog/ranking-factors-2013.

But you don't have to be on every platform in order to maximize your promotion potential; you only need to focus on platforms that reach your target audience.

Here is the list of social media platforms along with their target audiences:[13]

- Twitter: Under the age of 50, mostly 18–29, both men and women
- Facebook: All ages, both men and women
- Tumblr: Ages 18–29, both men and women
- Instagram: Ages 18–29, both men and women
- LinkedIn: All ages, both men and women
- YouTube: All ages, mostly 25–34, both men and women[14]
- Pinterest: Ages 18–64, mostly women
- Reddit: Ages 18–24, mostly men

Go back to the branding worksheet you created in the previous section and take a look at your target audience. Identify the social media platforms they utilize and focus your energy there.

Keep in mind that different social media platforms serve different purposes. While your target readership may be on Facebook and Pinterest, you don't want to ignore

---

13 Irfan Ahmad, "#SocialMedia 2014: User Demographics for Facebook, Twitter, Instagram and Pinterest – #infographic," *Digital Information World*, October, 13, 2014, http://www.digitalinformationworld.com/2014/10/social-media-user-demographics-linkedin-tumblr-facebook-and-more-infographic.html. Maeve Duggan, Nicole B. Ellison, Cliff Lampe, Amanda Lenhart, and Mary Madden, "Demographics of Key Social Networking Platforms, *Pew Research Center: Internet, Science & Tech*, January, 9, 2015, http://www.pewinternet.org/2015/01/09/demographics-of-key-social-networking-platforms-2/.

14 Eric Blattberg, "The Demographics of YouTube, In 5 Charts," *DIGIDAY*, April 24, 2015, http://digiday.com/platforms/demographics-youtube-5-charts/.

Twitter, since most booksellers, librarians, and media professionals utilize the platform. If you're targeting the teens on Instagram and Tumblr, you won't want to overlook their parents, who probably use Facebook and Pinterest.

CONTENT

Once you've identified the social media platforms you will focus on, it's time to develop a content strategy. Some authors may just post whatever is on their mind, but the ones who really utilize the platform will have a content strategy.

Refer back to the topics and talking points you created in the branding portion of the book. This should serve as a guideline for what sort of branded content to post. Remember, this isn't promotional content. We'll get to that later. This is original, interesting content that draws in potential readers and demonstrates who you are and how you write without directly telling people.

Topics

Open a new document or take out a sheet of paper and write out your tagline or author brand description you created earlier. Then, start listing types of content you could post to social media that would fall in line with you and your brand.

Stick to topics that are on brand and appeal to your target audience. Use a consistent voice that's a mixture of your real voice and your writing voice. For example, if you write with a southern dialect but don't have one yourself, try mixing in some southern slang while keeping the voice in formal English.

Promote Without Promoting

You're probably looking at this list and thinking, "Great, but when do I get to talk about my book?" The answer is sparingly.

As a guideline, I recommend rotating through 3 different types of posts:

1. Personal
2. Promotional
3. Interactive

Personal posts don't mean instagramming photos of every meal you consume or tweeting every thought that enters your mind; they should all relate to the topics outlined above. Personal posts can be notes about your writing process, articles from your research, books you're reading, movies you're watching, etc. They are meant to give readers insight into you as a person, while maintaining your online persona and voice.

Promotional posts are those relating to your book or yourself as an author. Promotional posts should *never* consist of the words, "Buy my book." No one likes a hard sell. Instead, try the following:

- Excerpts and quotes from your book
- Links to and blurbs from positive reviews
- Updates about events and signings

- Photos when your books are spotted at bookstores, are being read on the train, etc.

This type of content should always be presented in a humble, so-excited-to-share sort of way. Read all promotional posts aloud to see if they sound braggy. Promotional content should feel like exciting news you're sharing with your followers rather than blatant self-promotion.

Interactive posts are those that engage other users. On Twitter, interactive posts refer to @ replies and RTs. On Facebook, it's likes, comments, and shares. On Pinterest, it's re-pinning, liking, or commenting. These posts put the networking in social network and show that you're an active member of the community.

If you post only promotional content, people will start un-following you because your feed is basically an online billboard. If you only interact, people will un-follow you because you're not posting anything original. If you post only personal content, you miss out on the whole reason you're on the social media platform in the first place. You want to rotate through each type of post on a regular basis.

Your frequency of posting will vary depending on the platform. I've included that frequency on the social media cheat sheet overleaf.

Again, this may seem daunting, but you don't have to come up with unique content for each platform. It's perfectly acceptable to cross-post content, as long as you tweak the wording slightly to fall in line with the language of that particular platform.

For example, say you want to post an article about *The*

Platform	Age Demographic	Gender Demographic	Type of User	Recommended Posting Frequency
Twitter	Under 50	Both	Movers and shakers (booksellers, librarians, media pros, industry pros)	3–5 times a day
Facebook	All ages	Both	General consumers	3–5 times a week
Tumblr	18–29	Both	More tech-savvy consumers	Twice a day
Instagram	18–29	Both	More tech-savvy consumers	Once a day
LinkedIn	All ages	Both	Business professionals, those interested in career development	3–5 times a day
YouTube	25–34	Both	General consumers	1–2 times a month
Pinterest	18–64	Mostly women	General consumers	3–5 times a week
Reddit	18–24	Men	More tech-savvy consumers, adult geeks	1–2 times a month

Girl on the Train becoming a bestseller. Here is how you would tweak your post to fit the various platforms:

TWITTER: Insight from @Goodreads on how THE GIRL ON THE TRAIN became a runaway success: [link]

FACEBOOK: I still haven't read THE GIRL ON THE TRAIN, but since the book launched in January, I've seen it everywhere. Check out this interesting article about how Goodreads played an integral role in the book's success: [link, with link preview]

LINKEDIN: Books don't hit the bestseller list because they're lucky. Books hit the bestseller lists because publishers market them in strategic and calculated ways: [link, with link preview]

It's the same content, just presented differently.

Networking

Many authors are so focused on promoting their books and building their following that they lose sight of social media's primary purpose: networking. At their core, all social media platforms are meant to connect people online. At Facebook's conception, it was about connecting college students. Instagram is about sharing cool photos with friends. LinkedIn is all about professional networking online. While businesses capitalize on these platforms to market their products, ultimately, social media is about making connections.

According to Nielsen data, twenty percent of readers report discovering new authors because a friend or family member recommends them.[15] Who's to say that friend or family member couldn't be someone who's connected to you on social media? By networking with readers, other authors, librarians, and booksellers, you are able to generate buzz and increase word of mouth.

The first step is to connect with these types of influencers from your various social media accounts. Start off by searching people from your email contacts (most social media platforms will offer to do this automatically when you sign up). Then, start plugging in author friends, your local bookstore, library, etc. Start with people and places you actually know. From there, take a look at who those people/places are following. Are there other authors you recognize? Librarians? Media pros? If successful authors are following them, there's probably a reason.

You are also able to perform organic searches for types of users and hashtags from any social media platform. Plug in keywords like "books" or "librarian" and the social site will search users' profiles for those keywords. You can also search for influencers using sites like Klout and FollowerWonk, but organic searches tend to work just as well.

Once you've followed enough people, your feed will be populated with content on a regular basis. Now you can move on to the second step: engaging in conversation. This falls under the "interactive" post category and can include commenting on posts, @ replying, etc., and should be done in an organic, natural way. Think of it as a conversation with a group of people; you wouldn't just stand there and

---

15 Nielsen's PubTrack Consumer, 2009–2013 (previously owned by Bowker).

listen to people talk—you would add your two cents. When someone posts something you can offer your opinion on, or offer another point of view or if you want to point them to another article they may be interested in, it's appropriate to offer that reply.

A good rule of thumb is to ask yourself whether or not your response is adding to the conversation and if it falls in line with your brand. If someone offers a political opinion that you disagree with, I wouldn't recommend voicing that opinion unless you write books with a political bent. And if your response is a simple "I agree" or "me too," then you're not really adding to the overall conversation—it's better to limit your interaction to liking or sharing it.

Make it a goal to engage with one new person each day. Soon, these users will become more than just people you follow; they'll be part of your network.

Social Media Management Tools

Still feeling overwhelmed by the posting schedule? There are several tools that will help streamline your content—and reduce the time you spend generating it:

HootSuite

This program allows you to monitor multiple social media accounts, schedule posts ahead of time, and respond to comments/messages without leaving the site. HootSuite supports Twitter, Facebook, LinkedIn, and Instagram. The free version allows you to update three accounts and there are several paid options, which support more accounts and offer analytics data. There's also an integration for Google Chrome and Mozilla Firefox so you can easily share content from around the web (similar to the "Pin It" button).

TweetDeck

This program is similar to HootSuite in that you can manage many accounts and schedule posts, but it only supports Twitter. If you only have one Twitter account, then I recommend using HootSuite, but if you're updating several Twitter accounts, then TweetDeck is a bit more streamlined.

Buffer

This is the most popular program among what we refer to as the "movers and shakers" in industries. Users who frequently link to articles and serve as aggregators for industry news favor Buffer. Like the previous programs, it allows you to schedule posts ahead of time and has an internet browser integration. It also offers more advanced analytics on the performance of your individual posts. However, you're unable to monitor your feeds, mentions, etc., like you are with the other platforms.

HubSpot

This paid program is a comprehensive marketing platform that has far more capabilities than social media management. It's able to analyze users and their relationship to your website (if they click on your Twitter profile, what they do after they click one of your links, etc.). However, most authors don't need such an extensive tool. If you write nonfiction and your ultimate goal is to gain more customers for your business, then HubSpot is something you may want to consider. But if you write fiction and you're just concerned about selling books, then it's not worth the return on investment.

IFTTT

If you're somewhat tech-savvy, then IFTTT (If This Then That) is a handy tool to manage your social media content as well as your other online platforms. This program allows you to create "recipes" that dictate how your apps behave. For example, you can create a recipe that says if you post a video to YouTube, then it will be shared on Tumblr. Or if someone tags you in a photo on Facebook, then it will be saved to your Dropbox or iCloud folders. It can be a bit more time consuming to set up and optimize, but everyone who uses IFTTT swears by it.

Feedly

While this isn't a social media management tool, it is a useful platform for generating new content. Instead of hunting down articles to post to social media, Feedly compiles the latest posts from blogs and websites you've preselected into one place and offers a preview of the content. You're able to sort the sites you've selected by category and easily find the type of content you're looking for.

As you can see, there isn't one tool that does everything. Each platform has different benefits. For most authors, HootSuite is the most comprehensive and easiest one to use. You can get by with having free accounts—just pick the three platforms that are the most important to you. But if you are trying to save as much time as possible, then the Pro version isn't a huge investment.

Depending on what you write, your goals for the book and your career, and your level of tech-savvy, these other platforms may be handy additions to your toolbox.

RESOURCES

Social Media Platforms

Twitter.com   YouTube.com
Facebook.com   Pinterest.com
Tumblr.com   Reddit.com
Instagram.com   Google+ (plus.Google.com)
LinkedIn.com

To locate influencers

Klout.com   FollowerWonk.com

Management Tools

HootSuite.com   HubSpot.com
TweetDeck.com   IFTTT.com
Buffer.com   Feedly.com

IN-PERSON BRANDING

Because we live in a digital age, most authors assume that all publicity, marketing, and branding can be done online and that there is little need to venture out of the house. They often believe that bookstores are crumbling and the age of nationwide book tours is over. But no matter how active you are online or how large your online following is, it is still necessary to take a shower, put on pants, and venture out into the real world.

Social media and other technological advances have not—I repeat, not!—replaced in-person networking. Instead, they've made it easier to build an audience and promote what you're doing out in the real world.

EVENTS

Most authors are expected to participate in events in conjunction with their book release. This can take the form of launch parties, bookstore and library signings, conferences, trade shows, live lit events, and book festivals. If you write for children, there are school visits and youth group talks. If you write business books, there are symposia, events where participants receive CLE credit, and other corporate functions. Many of these can assist you in promoting your book and your brand, but not all are the best use of your time. No type of event should be ruled out, but it's important to scrutinize each opportunity and avoid the temptation to say yes to every speaking invitation that comes to you.

Bookstore Readings or Signings

Every published author who has gone on tour will have horror stories from the road. Most of them will recall memories of arriving at a bookstore to see only two people sitting in the audience, one of those people being the bookstore employee. Standard bookstore and library signings can be brutal.

So, why even bother?

When authors tell me their horror stories, I assume one of three things went wrong:

1. They went to a location where they didn't have a network of fans, friends, and family that would attend the event.
2. The location did not have a built-in audience.
3. There was an act of nature or competing event that caused a drop in attendance.

In most cases, one of the first two things went wrong. Or both. Gone are the days when people would head down to their local bookstore each week to catch an author they've never heard of talk about their new book. Instead, they're at home watching Netflix, or on Twitter chatting with the authors they've actually read, or going to one of the many concerts, movies, and other events competing with that bookstore signing. The people who show up to bookstore signings are your friends, family, and die-hard fans. If that community of people doesn't live within a 30-minute drive of your event, no one is showing up.

When considering whether or not to schedule bookstore events around the launch of your book, the most important things to consider are locations. Create a list using the following criteria:

1. Geographic location: Where in the country do you have a large network of friends and family? How easy is it to get there? (Do you have to fly with connections? Are you able to stay with friends or do you need a hotel?)

2. Venue: Is the bookstore a successful retail establishment? Do they frequently host events? Will they continue to hand-sell your book after the event? Do they have a strong online retail platform?

3. Media potential: Is there an opportunity for media appearances in conjunction with your event? An author coming to town isn't news in New York or LA, but in places like Charleston, South Carolina or Boise, Idaho, it might be! It's particularly true if you've ever lived in that city.

Create a list of geographic locations asking yourself the first series of questions. Think of all the friends and family that could potentially attend your event and come up with a number of people you'd invite. Then take half that list and assume that's who will come. So, if your list contains 60 people, assume that 30 of them will show up. Also, consider how many of those people would buy the book even if you didn't have an event. Your mom, brother, daughter, and best friend will definitely buy your book, but your colleagues from work or cousins may only pick it up if there's a party attached to it.

Highlight the locations where at least 30 people will attend and the majority of those people will only buy the book if you host an event. Most likely, your list just got significantly shorter.

From there, search for potential venues in those geographic locations. IndieBound has a database of independent bookstores, which you can search by zip-code. Barnes and Noble can work as well, but only if they're accustomed to hosting events and open to having authors coordinate their own.

Go to the bookstore's website and see what types of events they host. If they regularly have events for top authors, it's a good sign that the store is worth pursuing. If they seldom host events or if it's mostly indie press and smaller authors, then you may want to pursue other options. Bestselling authors wouldn't visit stores that didn't have an audience or weren't savvy about hosting events. Follow the pros.

Once you've identified the key booksellers in your location, make a note of whether or not there is media potential in that area. If it's a big city with lots of competition for stories, then maybe not. On the flip side, if it's an extremely small town without its own set of radio and TV shows, then it may not be great either. But if it's in a medium-sized city—Omaha, Kansas City, El Paso, etc.—there's a good chance you'd be able to book a radio or TV show while you're in the area.

Take a look at your list now. Compare it to when you started. Most likely, you've narrowed it down to just your hometown. See why nationwide book tours are falling out of fashion?

Conferences

Usually organized by professional writing organizations, conferences range from small one-day events with a few hundred people to mammoth, four-day, multi-panel tracks with thousands of attendees. The upside to speaking at conferences is that there can be a huge built-in audience and you don't have to rely on your friends and family to show up. The downside is that you're competing with dozens, sometimes hundreds of other authors doing the same thing.

Most conferences are set up the same way: authors register for the conference (yes, you do need to pay a fee) and request to be placed on a panel. Depending on the conference, there may also be an opportunity to pitch a workshop. There are usually two to five programs running at the same time, and the panels are made up of three to five authors, plus a moderator. Some conferences support solo talks and workshops for authors and industry professionals with expertise in relevant areas, and there's usually a handful of headlining authors who get solo interviews.

Too often, I see authors get fixated on their panel placement: is it at a good time, is it a good topic, are the other panels at the same time more interesting, etc. But the panel presentation is not the only purpose for attending conferences.

Because conferences attract a greater number of authors, they also attract more booksellers, librarians, bloggers, and other people who can generate buzz for your book. There's also an opportunity to network with other authors, which is very important. You never know when you'll need a blurb or social media boost or book tour buddy. Lastly, the fans who attend conferences usually attend every year. There's an opportunity to build relationships with readers and develop those relationships over time.

As an aspiring author, you were probably focused on attending writing conferences and workshops that focused on craft or the process of getting an agent. Now that you're a published author, you want to target fan conferences and conventions, which will reach more readers. Examples of these include:

- Bouchercon World Mystery Convention
- San Diego Comic Con
- RT Booklovers Convention
- YALLFest
- Dragon Con

Most of these are genre or age-group specific, which helps for ensuring you reach the target audience. Conferences like Bouchercon and RT move to a different city each year, while Dragon Con and San Diego Comic Con are in the same location each year. While conferences have built-in audiences, location still plays a part in deciding which events to participate in.

Start out by Googling "writer's conference" or "book convention" and see what comes up. Add the ones that have potential to your spreadsheet, including name, URL, location, and any notes about the conference. Then, look at authors similar to you and see which conferences they're attending in the coming year. If you belong to a professional writing organization like Mystery Writers of America or Sci-Fi Fantasy Writers of America, go to that organization's website and look for a list of sanctioned conferences and events. If the conference has sponsorship from a professional writing organization, it's a good sign. You can also visit the website UpcomingCons.com and search conventions in your area and read reviews of past events.

Once you have your list, talk to your author friends, agent, and other industry folks to see which ones they think are worthwhile. You may receive different opinions on whether or not the conference was worth the time and money, but if you ask the right questions, you should be able to determine whether or not it's a good fit for you:

- Was the conference well run? Did you have issues with scheduling, figuring out the program, etc.?
- On average, how many people attended each panel?
- Were the panels focused on readers or were they more industry related?
- Was the book room busy? Signing lines long?
- Did you meet any booksellers, librarians, or bloggers?

If you just ask an author whether or not a conference is worth attending, they may say no because they didn't get on a panel, or yes because they had a fun time (even if it wasn't very productive). "Is it worth it?" will yield a subjective opinion, while these other questions will provide actual information.

Book Festivals

Book Festivals are similar to conferences in that there are usually multiple panels and talks, and a large amount of authors vying for attention. But most book festivals boast a few key differences.

The first, and main, one is that they're free. Book festivals tend to be supported by community grants, media sponsors, and vendors who pay to have booths in the exhibitor area. While conferences attract the super-fans who are willing to spend money to meet dozens of their favorite authors, book festivals attract a more diverse population. The super-fans come out too, but there are many festival attendees who come out to browse the book dealers and listen to a handful of authors. If there was a fee, they'd probably skip it, and since most book festivals are outside, so much depends on the weather.

Another key difference is that most book festivals are open to all genres. While most of them tend to have a literary bent, more and more festivals are putting together mystery, romance, and other genre panels. There are also a large number of festivals that focus only on teen and children's lit, but most standard book festivals boast a hefty amount of children's programming. After all, what better way to attract a wider audience than free outdoor story time for families?

While conferences usually consider all registered, published authors for panels, there is usually a more rigorous selection process for book festivals. The submission process begins well in advance of the event—up to nine months earlier. There is usually a committee that selects keynotes, featured authors, and panelists. If you're vying for a slot in the lineup, make contact with the programming director early.

If you don't receive a speaking slot, there are often opportunities to sign with bookstore vendors and writing organizations exhibiting at the festival. Look at the list of exhibitors and see if there's anyone you have a relationship with or who would be open to having you sign at their table. The local chapter of your writing organization or your local bookstore is often a good backup.

The major book festivals include the *Los Angeles Times* Festival of Books, Brooklyn Book Festival, Miami Book Fair International, Atlanta Journal-Constitution Decatur Book Festival, Texas Teen Book Festival, and Printers Row Lit Fest in Chicago. There are hundreds of others around the country, and while they may be smaller than the major players, it's a great place to start. Our authors have had very productive appearances at the Fox Cities Book Festival, Arkansas Literary Festival, Wordstock, and Utah Humanities Book Festival. Start local and work your way out.

Trade Shows

Unlike book festivals, which are consumer facing events, trade shows are geared toward people in the industry.

Because trade shows are industry facing, these are usually events your publisher will submit you to. When you start the marketing and publicity conversation with your in-house team, ask them if you're on their submission list to any of the trade shows. Emphasize your willingness to travel and even pay your own way there. Speaking and signing at these events is a great opportunity to build your brand, and it would be worth your time and money.

The most notable trade show in the book world is BookExpo America (BEA), held annually in New York, though it now plans to move to different cities every three years. This is where publishers from around the world exhibit their upcoming titles, agents meet with foreign publishers to negotiate foreign rights sales, and librarians and booksellers have the opportunity to scout out talent for their upcoming events. Attendees consist of media professionals and those who work within the publishing industry, not the general public, so the purpose of attending is different than other events. Trade shows are primarily used for networking and generating early buzz for the book among booksellers, librarians, and other people within the industry, not direct sales.

In addition to BookExpo America, there are smaller regional trade shows around the country including the Northern California Booksellers Association (NCBA), Southern Booksellers Association (SBA), and others. These are a bit more accessible than BEA, as there is a regional focus. Publishers tend to showcase only their top authors at BEA, but there's a chance they would submit you to the regional trade show in your area, especially if you're able to get there on your own. I always recommend speaking to your publisher about this possibility.

While BEA and the regional ABA shows focus on

booksellers, there's also the American Library Association (ALA) conferences, which focus on librarians. There are two main ones: ALA Annual and ALA Midwinter. There are also regional ALA trade shows around the country. If your books do well in the library market, or librarians are a part of your target demographic, then I recommend adding these shows to your list.

If you are self-publishing, I don't believe that these conferences are worth the return on investment. Since trade shows are aimed at those who work in bookstores and libraries, two places your book probably won't be available, you wouldn't be reaching anyone in your target audience. I recommend focusing on consumer facing shows instead.

Just as there is "off-the-book page" media coverage and "out-of-the-bookstore" events, there are also plenty of trade shows that target people outside of the book industry. If your book has one of those hooks, then I recommend researching and submitting yourself to those shows. For example, if you write about business management and small business marketing, trade shows targeting CPAs, attorneys, and medical practitioners could be good opportunities for getting your name out there and reaching new readers. If you write about food or cooking, there are plenty of trade shows targeting chefs, grocery retailers, and food-industry people. Again, think about your target audience. They may not be going to BEA or ALA, but they may be attending the CPA Society conference or the World Food Expo.

Live Lit Events

In most major cities, there has been a surge in live literature events which combine writing, storytelling, and performance, often in non-traditional venues. These events usually are more high energy and less formal than the old-school traditional salons or reading series. Most happen monthly and often center on a theme—confessions, moments of reckoning, childhood memories, etc.—and showcase a handful of seasoned writers, comedians, or storytellers who either read their work aloud or tell their stories off book. Not everyone is cut out for live lit, and not all material is appropriate, but if you have a good stage presence and a story that fits in with the theme, these events may be worth pursuing.

Note that most are not open mics—the lineups are almost always curated ahead of time. Also, it helps immensely to visit the shows you're considering ahead of time to meet the producers and hosts and help determine the type of audience they draw and the styles of storytelling that particular audience tends to enjoy.

Since live lit is more about the performance than the individual storytellers, many events have a large built-in audience. People go regardless of who's reading because they know what types of stories they're going to hear and are confident the performers have been vetted. Because of this, you don't have to scrounge up as many of your own attendees. And since most events showcase multiple authors, each person will pull in their small network, which leads to a cross-pollination of potential new fans.

While these live performances reach a new audience and are quite the rush for you as the author, they don't usually generate a lot of book sales. The regulars are there to see a performance, and don't necessarily have an interest in adding to their to-be-read pile. Most live lit events don't even bring in a bookseller to provide books; any authors who want to sell copies have to do so themselves.

So what's the point of doing these events if they don't result in book sales? Most of the time, there isn't a point. Rarely do we incorporate live lit events into an author's tour. But for our authors who have a stage presence and whose work is perfect for the bar scene, there are some advantages:

- Expand name recognition – Even if the attendees don't buy your book that night, they still hear your work and see you perform. Later in the week, they may hear you on the radio, or their Amazon account will suggest they might like your book. It's another impression.

- Media – Most live lit series are hooked in with the media, and if it's a regular event, they're often covered in the event listings section of your local newspapers and websites. While not everyone who reads the paper will come to the event, they're still seeing your name in a place they wouldn't otherwise.

- Meet influencers in the community – Some of the more prominent shows attract radio and podcast producers, local indie publishing reps, media reporters, authors, and other active members of the literary scene; and as a featured author you have the opportunity to establish mutually beneficial relationships.

- Bonus event – There have been many times when our authors were traveling for vacation or a conference and they wanted to maximize their trips. If an author doesn't have a new book out or a network of fans in that area, a bookstore or library event doesn't make sense. But if there's a local live lit series with a built-in audience willing to add the author into their lineup, it's a way for them to reach a new audience (and turn their vacation into a business trip, for tax purposes!).

As a consumer, I'm a huge fan of live lit. I think it's a fun night out and can be far more entertaining than a play or a movie. In the many years I've attended these events, I can count on one hand the amount of books I purchased from the readers, but that doesn't mean I didn't buy their books in the future. So while it doesn't make sense for all authors and shouldn't be done in lieu of a launch party or other bookselling event, there are occasions where reading at a live lit series is worth your time.

School Visits

If you write for children, tweens, and teens, school visits are going to be an important part of your campaign. School visits can be very rewarding and productive, if done correctly.

The best way to set up school visits is through your local bookstore. Most children's buyers have relationships with the area schools and work closely with them to ensure they stock books that coincide with the curriculum. And since book sales are a part of any school visit, it's in the bookstore's best interest to organize the largest possible events in markets where the students will purchase books.

This is another reason to do bookstore events. Often, if

you schedule a signing there that evening, the bookstore will schedule school visits for you during the day.

If the bookstore in your area won't set these up on your behalf, then you'll have to schedule them yourself. Researching schools and finding the appropriate contact information can be time consuming, so here are some tools to help with your search:

Start with schools that are in your area or that you have a personal connection to (you went there; you have a friend that teaches there, etc.).

Your best contact will be the school librarian or media specialist. After that, you can try for the English department head or one of the principals. Contacting individual teachers may get you scheduled for a class visit, but that means you're only reaching 20 or so students. You want to make sure you make the visit worth your time and connect with as many students as possible—preferably at least 50.

If you're not familiar with the school, plug it in to greatschools.org and see what type of rating and reviews it receives. If it's lower on the scale, they are probably facing too many other challenges to consider bringing in a speaker.

If you're planning on traveling to other locations for signings, conferences, or even vacation, I encourage you to check out the area schools and see if there's an opportunity to pay them a visit. Making personal connections is the best way to reach the 17-and-under crowd.

If you're visiting high schools or middle schools, you will want to ask for a school assembly, with multiple classrooms present. If that's not a possibility, a media center visit— where they can bring in 50–80 students—is still worth your time. Some teachers will ask for you to do classroom visits, which is more time consuming and draining, but if you're just starting out and it's a good school, then you may have to make it work. Avoid anything that requires a lot of work and time on your part without the return.

If you write for younger children, classroom visits or story time in the library may be your best option. There is no way to command a room of 100 eight-year-olds.

In most instances, I recommend preparing a 20-to-25-minute presentation using PowerPoint or Keynote. While there are many students who are interested enough to sit still and listen to someone talk for 45 minutes, most kids need visuals to guide them through and keep them engaged. Going back to your brand and talking points, think about what presentation would engage your audience and attract new readers.

Sample presentations include:

- It's Alive! Building Characters That Leap Off the Page (Heidi Schulz, *Hook's Revenge*)
- How I Became a Writer (Susan Dennard, *Truthwitch*)
- Technology from Science Fiction That's Actually Real (Lydia Kang, *Control*)

Create your own list of topics and descriptions of what the presentation will entail. I also recommend creating different versions for different age groups.

Remember, book sales should be a component of every school visit. If the local bookstore won't set up the event on your behalf, they will usually facilitate book sales. Since most middle schoolers and high schoolers don't walk around with a lot of cash on hand, the bookstore will usually send order forms home in advance of the event so students can place their orders and have the books ready for them at the school. This is the best way to maximize sales because it allows students to ask their parents to buy the book for them, rather than counting on them to use their own cash for the purchase. It also helps you anticipate the crowd and enthusiasm for the school. If you have a huge book order, you can expect an enthusiastic group of attendees. If the order is small, you may want to bring candy to bribe them into participating in the discussion.

Out-of-the-Bookstore Events

These unique and creative events can be the most fun to brainstorm and plan, but are often the most difficult to execute. As I've mentioned several times throughout this section, it is very difficult to get people out of their house and drive through traffic to an event. You're competing with movies, concerts, theater, and a million other local entertainment options. But what if your event was the most interesting happening thing in your area?

Over the years we've worked on dozens of unique events like this. They have included:

Literary Salons

Based on the literary salons of the 1700s and 1800s we brought together a group of panelists to discuss a topic. The inaugural event was, "Does Monogamy Kill the Soul?" and included a genetics expert, a Kabbalist, and two married comedians. It was held in a restaurant, so there were drinks and appetizers, and it was billed as "the thinking person's night out."

Books & Beer Holiday Shopping Night

We held this event in early December and marketed it as a way to find the perfect gift—a signed autographed book—for everyone on your list and have a beer while doing it. We had a variety of authors, each of whom write in different genres, in an effort offer something for everybody, and the authors were on hand to sign and personalize the books.

Chicago Literati Networking Event

This is the event we're best known for and have been organizing for nearly four years. Created with the idea of replicating the hotel bar at any writer's conference, the Literati event is an evening of networking with authors, booksellers, and publishing pros. There is no program but there are featured guests so attendees have a touchstone of whom to expect at the event. The first 30 people to register receive swag bags or books and other literary-themed goodies.

Cross-Discipline

There are authors who team up with bands and hit the road for a combination of music and live lit. Authors who write about food collaborate with restaurants and stores to provide cooking demos and classes. Some coordinate with wineries or distilleries to combine a tasting and signing. The possibilities are endless, as long as you keep a few things in mind:

- No matter what the event, there should be some element of book sales. If people can't buy your book or learn about your book, what's the point?
- It should be a unique, fun event that people will

want to go to. Anything with the words "lecture" or "talk" in the title tends to turn people off.

- The event should reach your target audience. If you're trying to reach middle schoolers, don't host an event in a bar. If you're trying to reach baby boomers, don't host an event that starts at 10 P.M.

If you are up to organizing one of these unique, "out-of-the-bookstore" events, I recommend joining forces with another author or two. This way, the burdens of planning duties and bringing in the audience won't all fall on your shoulders. While these take a lot more effort and planning, they can often yield the biggest return.

YOUR PUBLIC PERSONA

I always tell clients, "It's my job to book the event and fill the seats. It's your job to sell the book." Securing events is only a piece of successful in-person branding; the bigger piece is winning over the audience.

Just as you shouldn't post *everything* about yourself on social media, you shouldn't reveal every part of yourself during public appearances. You may spend most of your time working from home in your pajamas or wear a suit and tie to your day job, but your author persona may call for a sport coat and jeans or a colorful dress. You may feel strongly about politics, or religion, or other controversial topics, but unless it's a part of your author brand, they don't have a place in your speeches or author talks. You should identify the key aspects of your author brand and embody those in all public appearances.

Attire

This is something almost all my authors ask before their first conference or TV appearance: What should I wear? It isn't surprising, since most authors spend the majority of their lives writing in pajama pants and T-shirts, while others go to day jobs where they dress to the appropriateness of that job.

You may be surprised, but your author uniform will vary based on what genre you're writing in and for what age group you are writing for. If you look at author photos or see authors at conferences, you should be able to identify patterns in what they are wearing.

I'm not a fashion expert, and there are plenty of exceptions to these rules, but if you're not confident in your personal style and need some guidance, here is the recommended attire for major genres:

Mystery/Crime/Thriller

For men, and women if they prefer pants, the standard get-up is jeans and a sport coat. Some authors do T-shirts underneath, others do button downs. No suits or ties. Women can also be effective in slim-cut dresses, preferably dark tones and no patterns. Authors in these genres want to exude coolness, confidence, and have an ease about them without being too casual.

Romance/Women's Fiction/Chick Lit

These genres allow authors to make a bigger "statement" with their fashion and style. Most authors in these genres are women, and most of these women opt for dresses, color, and lots of patterns. Some will dress according to the subgenre they write in. It is common to see authors who write Western romance to dress in cowboy boots and denim. Authors who write millionaire romances or about female executives trying to balance work and love may opt for a business suit or a skirt and button down. If you happen to be a man writing in these genres, I recommend following guidelines for the crime fiction authors. As a man writing in a woman's world, you don't need to stand out more than you normally do.

Literary Fiction/Historical Fiction/Academic Work

Since many authors in these genres tend to be college professors, they often dress like college professors. If you write in these genres, you could go a little nerdier and opt for more browns and tans, maybe even a bowtie. Think of what you would wear to teach a course in the English department and go with that.

YA and Middle Grade

This can be a tricky one to gauge, and some of it will depend on what you write and what the appearance is. First and foremost: You never want to be more casual than the students. If they're wearing jeans, you want to wear slacks or a skirt. If they have a uniform and the teachers wear suits, then go for a suit. That being said, I also recommend making more fashion-forward or bolder choices. Teens will notice a cool pocket square or unique necklace, and you'll be more memorable for it. I know many authors who have signature pieces (chunky rings, funky socks, etc.) that they wear to every signing to make themselves more memorable.

Sci-Fi/Fantasy/Comics and Graphic Novels

This is where you can break out the ironic T-shirts and Chuck Taylors. In these genres, it's better to align yourself with the fans than it is to set yourself above them. Showing that you too are a sci-fi or comics geek will help attract readers and build your fan base.

Business Books

If you're trying to attract the corporate crowd, then you need to dress like them: business professional. Certain accents will depend on the industry you're trying to reach (lawyers always wear ties, tech people never do, etc.).

For other genres not listed here, my advice is to think about what brand you're trying to establish, and then identify the look that will convey that brand. In my case, I'm a publishing professional, so I want to dress slightly more formally than my author counterparts, but I'm also in PR, so I want to demonstrate my creativity. That's why I tend to wear bowties, funky socks, and cool shoes. If you're a diet and fitness expert, you could get away with wearing workout clothes that show off your sculpted arms and six-pack abs. If you're a psychologist with a self-help book, then you want more comfortable, inviting clothing. When you walk in front of an audience, you should be conveying your brand through your appearance.

Speech and Tone

Your clothes will make the first impression, but you then need to open your mouth and talk about the book. For some authors, this is the part that comes naturally. They can talk about their writing process, books they love, and their recent release easily, without even thinking about it. Others have a tougher time and need to be coached on their talking points, audience engagement, and delivery. And like your attire, the way you speak to an audience will vary based on your author brand.

Think back to the authors you've seen speak over the years, which ones were the most memorable? Why? Did they have an ease about the way they spoke? Or were they blunt and direct? No matter the answers, chances are they are consistent for every group they speak to.

If you've never done public speaking before, I encourage you to practice your presentation and video record it. When you play it back, notice which parts are the most engaging, in which parts you are most animated, and which parts you struggle through. Analyze your own speaking style; try to amplify the strong parts and quell the weak ones. If you gesture a lot and get really animated, but sometimes go off on a tangent or lose your train of thought, then focus on staying on point and using those gestures as cues rather than distractions. If you tend to be more deadpan and don't have a lot of emotion in your voice, then play it up and amplify it by having really engaging content. Comedians like Mike Birbiglia and Jim Gaffigan have made a career doing deadpan comedy. It can work.

I encourage you to keep filming your speaking engagements. If the piece is very good you can use it for marketing purposes; if it's not quite there yet, you can still use it to analyze and improve your speaking—and to see how much you're improving with practice. Like a football coach analyzing game footage, it's important to review your mistakes so you don't repeat them. It's also important to see where the audience laughed, where they were zoning out, and where they had lots of questions, and to consider tailoring your talk for the next time around.

Above all, your speech and tone should be accessible to your target audience. If you use profanity in your books, it's okay to curse *occasionally* when you're talking to readers, but if you write traditional mysteries or sweet romances with no foul language, then using profanity in your talk will alienate your readers. Language is also important to consider when talking to teens. Clearly, they use profanity and slang, but since you don't want to position yourself as their peer, it's a good idea to avoid cursing and slang when speaking to that age group.

What You Talk About (and What You Don't)

Just because you *can* speak on a topic doesn't mean you should. In the branding section, you developed a clear list of talking points and facets of your brand you wanted to highlight. Throughout your career, there will be discussions, news stories, and trends that arise that you may be tempted to offer your opinion on. If speaking on these subjects falls in line with your brand, then you should utilize those opportunities, but if the subject matter is outside of that scope, then you should avoid offering your opinion.

For example, we work with many multi-published authors who have won awards, hit the *New York Times* and *USA Today* bestseller lists, made film deals, switched publishers, and overall, have a lot of experience in the publishing industry. There are many discussions about the future of bookstores, e-books, utilizing social media, and unique marketing efforts. They have a lot of knowledge in these areas and could add a great deal to these discussions.

But they don't. Because it is not a part of their brand.

In an effort to position these authors as the creative talent, they will speak on the creative process, other books they're excited about, and what makes a great story, but they won't speak on the business of publishing or its future. I want them to be known for their books and their writing talent, not their business savvy.

Now, if you're a business author, that's a whole other story. You *need* to be an expert in your field.

Your branding worksheet should give you a clear outline of your expertise and topics to include in your talk. Again, if you're an MBA or a CPA or a CMO, you probably have a lot more experience and knowledge than what is included on your branding worksheet. But if it's not part of your brand, then it needs to stay out of your talk.

For the most part, I recommend adhering to dinner party rules: no talk about sex, politics, and religion. No matter what side you're on, you'll alienate half (or more) of your audience. Exceptions are made for authors who write about these topics, but if there is no part of your book that addresses these issues, avoid them in all public appearances. If you follow the same guidelines as you do for your social media content, you'll stay on brand and attract your target audience.

So what do you talk about?

The content of your speech or talk will often depend on the audience. A bookstore appearance will be less formal than a fundraiser or library luncheon. How you address a book club, a group that's already read the book, will be different than at an event where you're trying to persuade attendees to buy the book. While the content of your talk may vary slightly depending on the audience, I recommend putting together a template for any upcoming appearances, based on the current book you're promoting.

The general talking points should be similar to those outlined on your branding worksheet, but here are some additional ideas you may want to incorporate into your public appearances:

- A funny or interesting anecdote about how you came up with the idea for this particular book
- A surprising discovery you made while researching the book or a cool thing you did in the interest of research (learn how shoot a bow and arrow, tour an industrial farm in Mexico, etc.)
- Little known facts about your writing process, and how they changed for this particular book
- Stories about the actual people you based some of the characters on

If you write nonfiction, you will likely already have a few formal talks based on the topics you write about. For example, this book stemmed from a workshop I've given for the past few years. If you've bought this book, you probably did it because you attended one of those workshops. By creating a presentation that offers a preview of the book, enough to pique people's interest but not so much that you give it all away, you're able to leave people wanting more, which results in them buying the book.

While I always recommend tailoring presentations to meet the needs of the audience, it's a good idea to have a canned presentation or two. This way, you'll be able to build a reputation and generate word of mouth, not only for the book, but for future speaking engagements as well.

NETWORKING

Events aren't the only types of public appearances you'll be making as an author; you'll also be expected to take advantage of networking opportunities. While there are some formal networking events, like the Chicago Literati, most networking opportunities occur in conjunction with formal events, and others come when you least expect it.

For formal networking events and any type of author event, come prepared to meet people and make connections. This includes:

- Wearing your "author uniform"
- Having plenty of business cards, bookmarks, and other small swag items
- Knowing your tag line or elevator pitch

I meet a lot of authors who attend these events with a mission: make a connection with a literary agent, meet booksellers, get introduced to a certain author, etc. But having tunnel vision means you may be missing out on meeting someone just as important.

There's a woman I know who's a former bookseller and voracious reader, and volunteers to help with programming for many of the mystery conferences. She tells me over and over again how authors come up to her, introduce themselves, and immediately try to gauge whether or not she's worth talking to. One even had the gall to ask her, "Are you someone important?" to which she responded with a shrug, "Just a reader." Immediately, the author's eyes darted around the room to see if there was someone else they should be talking to, when one of the most important people they could be connecting with, a reader who devours several books a week, was standing right in front of them. Not only is she a potential book buyer, but she's an influencer in the community and could recommend the book to other conference-goers she knows—that is, if she's met and liked the author.

When walking into a networking event or through a book festival, you should treat everyone you meet as a worthwhile contact. They may just be a midlist author like yourself, but midlist authors often hit bestseller lists. Or they may be a great critique partner. Or touring buddy. You may meet a book blogger who is just starting out, but in a few months that blogger could be a reviewer for a trade publication or their local newspaper. If you make a good impression, or a bad one, they'll remember you when your book comes across their desk.

To make a good first impression and lay the foundation for building a relationship, always start with making eye contact, introducing yourself, and shaking hands. That physical connection makes a difference. If you are walking into a group where you know some people but not others, say hi to the people you know, then introduce yourself to the people you don't. It's my pet peeve, and I suspect others' too, when people walk into a group of people and start talking to someone in the group individually without pulling them aside or introducing themselves to everyone else. However, don't be afraid to join in the group conversation, especially if you're somewhere that's set up for networking. When you walk into the hotel bar at a conference, you'll see small groups of people scattered around the room. Don't be afraid to hop into one.

Once you've introduced yourself, I always recommend focusing on the other person or people in the group. Ask questions that demonstrate you're listening and genuinely interested in what they have to say. I was once at an event when I was introduced to one of the new publishing reporters at the *Wall Street Journal,* an important contact for a book publicist to make. We talked for about 30 minutes. Well, he talked. I just kept asking him questions and let him talk the whole time. We swapped business cards, and when I followed up the next day, he wrote back saying that I was the most interesting person he talked to at the party. We've worked together on a handful of stories since then.

People love talking about themselves, and most don't get to do it too often. Don't be afraid to shine the light on the other person, and don't be so consumed with making a first impression that *you're* the one who talks the entire time. Letting someone hog the mic can make a better impression than keeping the mic to yourself.

But eventually, most people will ask the inevitable question, "So, what do you do?" or "What do you write about?" At this point, you should have your tag line or elevator pitch locked and loaded:

"I write women's fiction that explores the
lengths people will go for their families."

"I write international thrillers in the
vein of Robert Ludlum."

"I write books to help individuals
become better managers."

Most people will follow up with questions that demonstrate they're listening and genuinely interested in what you have to say, at which point it's fine to talk a bit about yourself. Just remember, conversation goes back and forth. Don't hog the mic.

Remember, you're trying to connect with many people, not just one or two. After talking to someone or a group of people for a good amount of time, you'll need to make a graceful exit. If you already have your eye on someone that you want to talk to, just say, "Excuse me, but there's someone I need to say hi to. It was really great meeting you!" Handshake. Eye contact. Smile.

If you're not sure who the next connection will be, then I recommend excusing yourself to use the restroom, grab another drink, or make a phone call. But make it genuine—don't say, "Sorry, I have to make a call," and then walk over to the person next to you. Take a step outside, look at your phone, then step back into the room and meet your next person. You can also use that moment looking at your phone as a way to inconspicuously scan the crowd and see who you want to meet next.

The final thing to remember, and the key element in making a genuine contact, is the follow-up. The day following the networking event or the conference, go through all the business cards you swapped and send a follow-up email. This should include the following:

- It was great meeting you at [insert event].
- One line demonstrating that you remember them and triggering their memory of you (So great to meet a fellow Michigan alum, loved swapping social media horror stories, etc.).
- A call to action or next step (Will you be at X conference? I'd love to connect about Y, etc.). Think of some ways to build the connection. Sometimes, it's offering help (saying you'll check out their book, or if an agent will be in your city, offering to take them around, etc.). It's always better to offer something before asking for something.

These general guidelines are tailored for conferences and networking events, but they work everywhere: dinner and cocktail parties, functions at your day job, even at the gym or community center. Remember, everyone is a potential reader, a potential fan, and you never know who you're going to meet. I've connected with clients through my swim team, street festivals in my neighborhood, even at friends' weddings. Wherever you go, wherever you meet new people, they will inevitably ask, "What do you do?" And if you follow the steps outlined above, you will secure a new connection, and possibly, a new fan.

RESOURCES

IndieBound.org

UpcomingCons.com

Left Coast Crime

Malice Domestic

San Diego Comic Con

New York Comic Con

C2E2

Dragon Con

Wizard World Conventions

RomCon

YALLFest

NOVA Teen

Texas Teen Book Festival

Decatur Book Festival

Brooklyn Book Festival

National Book Festival

Printer's Row Lit Fest

Bay Area Book Festival

Utah Humanities Festival

Fox Cities Book Festival

Arkansas Literary Festival

Baltimore Book Festival

BookExpo America

GreatSchools.org

Chicago Literati Networking Event

Bouchercon World Mystery Convention

Romance Writers of America Annual Conference

RT Booklovers Convention

Los Angeles Times Festival of Books

Miami Book Fair International

American Booksellers Association

American Library Association

ADDITIONAL PROMOTIONS

The best aspect of my job is that no two campaigns are exactly alike—every book, every author, is unique. We don't take a plug-and-play or a one-size-fits-all approach, and therefore we strive to bring at least one unique marketing or advertising idea to every campaign we execute. This is what has set us apart from other PR companies, and this approach is what can set your book apart from the rest. If you execute everything outlined in the previous chapters, your chances of successfully launching your book are pretty high. But by incorporating a little something extra, your odds get even better.

There are a lot of marketing tools, terms, and buzzwords out there. Fellow authors will tell you about all the things you *have* to do to market your book, or a friend of yours in consumer marketing may drill into you that X or Y is the "next big thing." The rules for marketing are the same as publicity: if it doesn't reach your target audience, then there's no point doing it. Certain initiatives may work for marketing

Coca-Cola or Lexus, but they won't work for selling books. When brainstorming marketing ideas, think about your target audience of readers and evaluate whether or not these efforts will reach them. Will these initiatives serve to complement your publicity efforts, making multiple impressions on the same group of people, giving them the feeling that they're seeing your book everywhere? If the answer to these questions is yes, then the idea is worth considering, as long as you have the time and the budget to do it right.

The promotions outlined in this section are by no means the complete list of the only ones worth doing. At Kaye Publicity we have firsthand experience with each of these campaigns and are sharing our experiences with you because we feel that they may add value to your promotional plan as well. If a marketing or advertising opportunity isn't listed here, that doesn't mean it isn't worthwhile; it just means we haven't tried it.

Any campaign comes with a certain amount of risk, but by asking the right questions and doing the proper research, you can minimize that risk. Not every idea that pops into your head is worth doing, and the latest marketing trend may not apply to you and your audience. But if there's potential to reach your target audience and earn a big return on your investment, then it's worth a shot. The only thing worse than failing is never having tried at all.

EMAIL MARKETING

This is one of the most underestimated promotion tools authors have at their disposal, especially if you're marketing to an older crowd. Not everyone is on Twitter, or spends a lot of time on Facebook, or reads the news online. But almost everyone, about 86.5% of the US population, has an email address.[16] They may rarely use it, but if an email is in their inbox, they'll see it, unlike Twitter and Facebook posts, which often get lost in the shuffle.

Services

There are a few email marketing services, some are free and some cost a small amount for every send. The one we use the most often is Mailchimp. It's easy to use, highly customizable, and free if your mailing list is under 2,000 subscribers. There is also TinyLetter, which happens to be a spin-off of Mailchimp, which is an emailing service that is more personal and has fewer business features and analytics. Many authors say they prefer TinyLetter because it feels more personal and less like blatant self-promotion. Other services include Constant Contact and Vertical Response, both of which are paid services (usually pay-per-email sent) and a bit more difficult to customize. Some users report their emails are less likely to get caught in spam with the services Constant Contact or Vertical Response than with Mailchimp, but I haven't had the experience of my Mailchimp messages being flagged as spam.

Building a List

Once you decide which service works best for you, create an account, create a list, and prepare a sign-up form. Add

16 "Internet Users," *Internet Live Stats*, http://www.internetlivestats.com/internet-users/.

the newsletter sign-up form to your website and Facebook page (most have a Facebook integration tool that makes it easy). Once a month or so, remind your Twitter followers to sign up for your newsletter and include a link. I also advise authors to roll it in with a contest—maybe everyone who signs up before a certain date will receive a signed bookmark and bookplate, or one lucky winner will receive an Amazon gift card. Whatever it is, hosting a contest will encourage people to sign up and you'll grow your list much faster.

Technically, people have to sign up for your mailing list themselves; you're not allowed to add people without their permission. Many authors will stick to that rule; others will ignore it completely and add every person they ever met or swapped business cards with to their mailing list. I believe the ideal approach is somewhere in the middle.

Create a spreadsheet of friends and family members you think will be interested in receiving your newsletter and won't be offended when it arrives in their inbox. Add any fans that have written you expressing interest in your work. If there are authors who have emailed you asking for a blurb or to read their manuscript or to connect them with your agent, add them to your list. My rule of thumb is that if they've expressed interest in you and your work, or if they've asked you for professional assistance, and they aren't likely to get offended by receiving an email from you, add them. They can unsubscribe if they want.

Do not add book critics who have reviewed your book, but have never written you separately. Don't add people you met at conferences and never corresponded with except to say, "Nice meeting you." If they wouldn't know you by name, they don't belong on your list.

Many of you won't feel comfortable doing that, and that's fine. But most of us in the industry expect to be added to authors' mailing lists, especially if we've written them in the past. To be honest, sometimes it's a nice surprise. If I meet an author at a conference, get their card, and email them to say, "Nice meeting you" or "I loved your latest book," I won't always go to their website and seek out a newsletter sign up. But if they add me and they don't send too many e-blasts, I definitely won't unsubscribe and I am grateful for the reminder when they have a new book out.

When to Send and What to Say

When it comes to figuring out frequency of emails and what to include in each, a lot of it is common sense: don't send emails every day, don't be overly promotional, and don't only send when you have a book out, but don't send emails when you really have nothing to say. There are a few different ways to execute email marketing effectively, but whatever you decide, I recommend sticking with it and remaining consistent. If you decide to send semi-monthly or quarterly newsletters, stick with that schedule. If you only send 3 emails a year when you're gearing up for a book launch, maintain that. Don't change it dramatically just because you have a book out or there's an initiative your publisher wants to promote. You train readers to know what to expect from you, and if you deviate too far from that expectation, you'll lose subscribers.

If you write multiple books a year, publish in multiple arenas, or just have a lot going on that would interest your subscribers, then I recommend a quarterly or semi-monthly newsletter. This will allow you to connect with your readers on a regular basis and provide new and interesting information with each email. If you write one book a year or less, and that's really the main focus of your email marketing, then you can opt to send 2–3 newsletters around your book launch, and that's it. For this, I recommend sending one 8 weeks out, one 4 weeks out, then one on launch day.

When scheduling an email marketing campaign, you also want to consider the date, day of the week, and time it's going out. About half of your subscribers will check their email at work, probably after they've cleared their professional inboxes. The other half will check it before they start their workday or in the evening when they return home. People's inboxes are the fullest on Monday morning and emails sent on Friday afternoon are often overlooked. You want to pick the optimal time for people to open and read your content, rather than when they're more likely to just delete the email because they're pressed for time and overwhelmed by the amount in their inbox.

I used to always send emails midday, thinking that people are less likely to delete messages when their inboxes have been cleared. But a recent study conducted by Boomerang for Gmail[17] revealed that email is 30% more likely to be opened if it's sent between 6–7 A.M. I started using this tactic in our own newsletters and right away we noticed an increase in open rates. I attribute this to the type of content we're sending; recipients may be more inclined to read a newsletter while they're brushing their teeth, waiting for the train, or having their first cup of coffee. Wait too long and

---

17 Boomerang, Nov 12, 2015. *Boomerang for Gmail Webinar Recording.* https:// www.youtube.com/watch?v=Rwv4cue9c5k&feature=youtu.be.

they've already started their day—they don't have time to read about your upcoming book.

I usually send emails Tuesdays–Thursdays, unless Monday or Friday is a holiday, in which case I send on Wednesday. Lastly, you want to avoid sending e-blasts during the week of spring break, Thanksgiving break, or other times of the year when people travel. Your message will likely get buried under the rest of unwanted and non-emergency emails, and eventually deleted.

The content of the newsletters will vary depending on the schedule, but the key rule is the same: be consistent. If your newsletters always include some personal anecdotes, photos from research trips, little known facts about the region you write about, etc., then keep that up. Some authors, like Susan Dennard, opt to send a more service-based newsletter that includes writing tips, prompts, and publishing information. If you prefer to keep it about the book, that's fine too. But it's awkward, not to mention jarring, for your readers to transition from writing humorous, anecdotal, first-person emails about your recent research trip to an all-business, straight–book-information type email.

If you're opting for the "only around the book launch" schedule, then I recommend including the following content in each newsletter:

- Newsletter #1 (8 weeks prior to publication day): A synopsis of the upcoming book, buy links, any early reviews, and tour dates.
- Newsletter #2 (4 weeks prior): Latest reviews of the book, a sample chapter or excerpt, tour schedule, buy links.

- Newsletter #3 (launch day): A simple announcement that the book is out, with buy links. Keep it short and sweet.

If you're aiming for more of an anecdotal or service-based newsletter, you'll still want to send out a launch day announcement with links to buy the book. Since you wouldn't have sent the previous two promotional newsletters listed above, I recommend including the tour dates, reviews, and an excerpt if available.

For all email blasts sent, you should ask yourself the question, "What benefit is the recipient getting from my newsletter?" The answer to that question should not be the privilege of receiving information about your book. Maybe it's writing tips or advice. Maybe it's extra content unavailable to the general public. In our newsletters, we give away free books with every blast. Whatever it is, there should be some tangible benefit for subscribing to your list. No one would sign up to receive an advertisement in their inbox each month.

WATTPAD

This platform originally launched as a place for writers, mostly teens, to publish fan fiction. Unpublished authors would post their works in progress on the platform and other users were able to critique their work, encourage them to keep going, or simply vote it up or down. Many users have managed to build a large following of readers before their books were even finished, let alone published, so it became known as a community setting that could help an unknown writer launch a career.

However, now that Wattpad has grown to include more than 40 million readers and writers, many established authors also use the site to generate buzz and attract new readers. There are many possibilities, depending on your content and audience, but here are two ways our team has utilized Wattpad to build our authors' brands:

Crowd-Sourcing Campaigns

Like Kickstarter and Fundly, which bring masses of people together to fund a project, a crowd-sourcing campaign brings readers together to advance your story. About four to five months ahead of your book launch, post the first 5 pages to Wattpad. On your homepage, as well as your social media pages, let your followers know that you'll post the next 5 pages if a certain number of them vote for the excerpt, or even just read it. This gives readers a responsibility; if they want to read more, they have to earn it. It will encourage them to share your content and get their friends to read your work, thus building a network of readers. Other than a few social media posts, it requires minimal effort on your part.

Linked Novella or Short Story

For the past few years, publishers have encouraged authors launching a new series or who have a lag in between books to publish a novella or short story linked to the world of their novels. The traditional strategy—which rarely works—is for publishers to release this content on Amazon for $0.99 or $2.99 prior to the new book's launch in the hopes of drawing in new readers. The reason it doesn't work is the same reason why many full-length books don't sell well: there's no audience. Throwing up a book on Amazon doesn't mean people are going to download it, even if it's free.

But Wattpad has a built-in audience of readers who are used to reading new work from unknown authors. These readers are much easier to reach than the browsers on Amazon.

If you have a deleted scene from your book, a story that happens before the start of the series or in between books, or a minor character you've always wanted to write a novella about, this is the perfect opportunity to build an audience before the book comes out. Again, other than a few social media posts, it requires minimal effort on your part.

With its large, influential community, Wattpad is a powerful tool, though it's not for every type of author. While there is a growing audience for chick lit and fantasy, the most popular categories by far are romance and teen fiction. If either of those are your genre, then you should be on Wattpad.

One final note is that, like any other social media platform, it's important to be an active participant. I'm not saying you need to spend time reading content on Wattpad, but if people are commenting on your work, make it a point to respond to those comments and engage with your followers.

GOODREADS

On paper, Goodreads seems like it would be the ideal tool for authors. It's an online community of readers who share what they're reading or want to read, rate and review books, and have online discussions. Authors are able to have a profile with all their books listed, host Q&As, and incorporate their latest blog posts and tour dates. Readers can become "friends" with the author or just follow their updates. By marketing to a Goodreads audience, you're reaching a captive audience of readers.

So why does the mention of Goodreads trigger a groan from so many authors and publishing pros? I believe there are two reasons.

First, many authors used Goodreads regularly as readers. They enjoyed keeping track of what they were reading, reviewing the books they finished, and being an active participant in the community. But as soon as they became a published author and their personal profile had the "Goodreads author" stamp across it, the expectations changed.

As an author, it's never a good idea to review other authors' books. If you're critical, it could hurt your relationship with that author and the book's publisher. Remember, you may be published by Penguin today, but you could easily be moved to Harper or Simon and Schuster tomorrow. Never burn your bridges. If you praise a book, your review could be taken as a blurb and used for future books, ones that you haven't read and aren't vouching for, which can hurt your brand in the long term.

Rating a book is okay, but only if you can honestly give

it five stars, the highest amount allotted. Anything less would be deemed as criticism and reflect poorly on you. That being said, I do recommend adding your favorite books to your bookshelf and giving them five stars, especially if readers who like those books would also like yours.

The second reason is that the Goodreads community can be vicious. Unlike retailer sites such as Amazon and Barnes and Noble, which only allow you to post a review after the book is out, Goodreads allows readers to post reviews as soon as the book is listed. There are many people who will review a book without having read it, just because they have a beef with the author or have an axe to grind. It can be brutal on an author to receive such negative feedback before the book is even out.

Whenever authors freak out to me about their Goodreads reviews, especially those prior to publication, I tell them this story. One of our authors called me, very upset, that he had received a two-star review on Goodreads. I told him to chill out, that it wasn't a big deal and they don't know what they're talking about.

"No, they really don't," he said, "because this review is for the book I haven't even finished yet."

I went online and sure enough, someone had already posted a page and a poor review for a book they couldn't possibly have read.

So, if Goodreads is such a hotbed of bitterness and negativity, then why even bother? Because even though there are many members who just want to complain, there are twice the number of readers who use Goodreads to discover new books. They may not always post the most in-depth reviews, but that doesn't mean they aren't reading.

When it comes to your Goodreads presence, I recommend the following:

- Claim your Goodreads author page (there is a link to do this from the home page)
- Keep your profile up to date with the most current author photo, official bio, and event information
- Add your favorite books and rate them five-stars
- Do not engage with readers and people who review your book. This is especially true for those who post negative reviews, but even readers who post positive reviews probably don't want to hear from you. It feels intrusive.

In addition to your author profile, Goodreads provides additional marketing opportunities, some worth more than others.

Giveaways

As a Goodreads author, you have the opportunity to host a sweepstakes, giving away copies of your book. Many publishers and authors give away advance reader copies (ARCs) prior to publication to generate early buzz and potentially secure early reviews. You can also give away finished copies once they're available. Until recently, giveaways were only available for physical books, so this promotion was unavailable to e-only authors, but in May, 2016, Goodreads announced that they will be offering this marketing promotion for e-books as well.

I find giveaways to be useful for a few reasons. First, they often prompt Goodreads users to add your book to their "shelves," their virtual "to-be-read" pile. Those who win those early copies will often review the book in advance of publication, which helps with generating early buzz. Lastly, if someone has your book on their to-read shelf and you create a giveaway, they will receive an email announcing that the book is available to win. This is free advertising, which creates additional impressions of your name and book cover.

What I see many authors getting wrong is the timing and amount of books being given away. The timing of the giveaway needs to be very strategic. For advance reader copies, I recommend scheduling the giveaway as soon as they're available and closing it three weeks later. This time period usually falls 4–5 months in advance of publication. This way, the winners will have time to read and review the book before it's out. If you're giving away finished copies, you can schedule the promotion closer to the publication date, but the giveaway should close at least two days in advance of your pub date. Everyone thinks they're a winner, and if they've entered to win a free copy of your book, that means they're going to hold off on buying it until the giveaway closes, just in case they win. You want your readers buying the book as soon as it's available, and closing the promotion prior to the pub date will help ensure that happens.

In terms of quantity, much of that will depend on book availability. If you have access to all the ARCs and finished copies you want, then I usually recommend offering 5–10 with each giveaway. More than that saturates the market and less than that decreases people's odds so much that they're discouraged from entering. I've seen a lot of publishers trying to generate early reviews by giving away dozens, sometimes even a hundred ARCs in advance of publication. I don't believe that tactic works. If the only purpose of giving away books is to generate early reviews, then you're better off relying on your newsletter or circle of friends to read the book and post their reviews. The percentage of giveaway winners who review the book is fairly low, so while giving away 5–10 will only yield a handful of reviews, it also doesn't break the bank or take hours to ship—and it raises awareness for the book in the process.

Advertisements

While I do not recommend this expenditure, there are those who believe it yields results, so we'll look at the two main advertising options Goodreads offers—and why I don't think they're worthwhile.

The simplest and most affordable is the self-serve advertising. These ads boast text and your book cover image, similar to the Facebook ads you see in the sidebar. These appear alongside your recommendations, but are clearly marked as "sponsored books." The self-serve ads don't require any graphic design and are pay-per-click, so they accommodate even a modest budget.

There are also larger display ads that are featured throughout the site. These are significantly more expensive and there is a minimum advertising budget, usually around $5,000. This does not include the ad creation, which you would need a graphic designer or creative agency for. These ads are more visually appealing and make a longer lasting impression.

Many authors and publishers swear by these ads, but

personally, I've never seen the return on investment. The self-serve ads don't receive the clicks and are often hidden at the bottom of pages or off to the side, so while they're affordable, they don't showcase or enhance your brand in any real way. The display ads, on the other hand, are seen by everyone and do make a longer lasting impression. However, I have a difficult time justifying the cost and I'm not really seeing the return on investment. Investing $5,000 means that, in the end, you have to reach somewhere around 10,000 new readers (more if you're traditionally published, fewer if you're self-published) to make it worthwhile. I understand that advertising seldom directly leads to purchases, but even so, it's hard for me to envision 10,000 readers seeing that ad, and seeing it in enough other places to make them buy the book.

We'll talk more about advertising later in the chapter, and there are types of advertising that do make a difference. But with Goodreads, I just don't see the value.

CONTENT MARKETING

Content marketing has been all the rage in recent years, especially among online business owners. This is where content that appears on your site, usually in the form of a blog post, is aggregated to other high-traffic sites around the web. When you finish reading an article on People.com or CNN.com you'll see a box of "Other articles that may interest you," with accompanying images. Clicking on those articles will take you off People or CNN and to another site where that article is published. Rather than enticing potential customers through advertisements (which most of us ignore), you're drawing people in through content that interests them.

Most authors and publishers haven't caught on to content marketing, but it's only a matter of time until they do. This is a low-cost way to drive a lot of traffic to your site and reach your target demographic.

The Players

There are two companies that are the primary players in content marketing: Taboola and Outbrain. Both these companies work the same way: you load the content you want to promote and upload the corresponding image, and you pay every time someone clicks on the article. There's usually a minimum buy for the year, but it's pretty low. They each offer different levels of support, and they will help you if your content is underperforming. The only major difference between the companies is the website partners. I recommend receiving lists of partners from both companies, reviewing those lists, and evaluating which is better for reaching your target audience.

Cision, the company we use for our media database, has also gotten into the content marketing game, partnering with both Taboola and Outbrain to reach the widest network possible. This sets them apart in that you can sign with one company and reach the list of two, but since they're playing middle man, it also means their pay-per-click rate is slightly higher. If you find that content marketing is really working for you and you want to do it on a larger scale, but you don't have time to manage multiple accounts, then you may want to pursue Cision. Otherwise, I recommend picking one of the two main players, reaching a smaller network of websites, and paying less per click.

The Strategy

Since the goal is to get people to click on your link, I see many companies using click-bait headlines that will entice people to click out of curiosity. This works to drive traffic, but in order to be effective, what you're selling needs to directly link to the content you're promoting. While the latest dirt on Kim and Kanye or ten ways to reduce belly fat may entice people to click, unless that's the type of book you're selling, it's not going to translate into sales.

As the phrase "content marketing" suggests, when it comes to a successful campaign, content comes first and the marketing comes second. Go back to your list of guest article topics and pick one or two that would appeal to a wide audience and have the most potential to be "clickable." Write those articles and post them to your blog or website. Make sure everything else on your website is up to date and that your book links and other important information is easy to find.

Once you have prepared the content, I recommend trying a variety of headlines to see which one generates the most click-throughs. For example, if I wanted to market the article Sophie Littlefield wrote about reinvention after divorce, I would try these headlines:

- "I reinvented myself after my divorce, and you can too!"

- Tips for starting over after divorce
- Reinvent yourself after divorce
- Bestselling author Sophie Littlefield talks reinvention after divorce
- Bestselling author on the secrets of starting over after a divorce

There are many more possibilities, but this is a good start. Using Taboola or Outbrain's self-serve platform, post each of these headlines with a link to your article and an accompanying image. I also recommend mixing up the imagery as this sometimes affects what people click. Once all of the links are loaded and approved, those articles will start feeding out to the various webpages.

After a week, take a look at which articles are performing the best. Most people just take a look at the click-throughs, but I also encourage you to look at the back end and see what those people do once they get to your site. If one headline has received 100 click-throughs, but the people who clicked from that headline don't click through to other pages on your site, then it may not be your top performer. Your top performing headline is the one where the most people click through and stay to read more of your content. If they click through to your books page or click one of the buy links, even better. Once you identify the top performers, I recommend pausing the rest of the campaigns and diverting all your funds there.

A few words on pay-per-click advertising: There are a lot of options out there, but content marketing has proved to be far more effective. We have grown increasingly immune to advertising and we tune so much of it out. On the flip side, we're reading more and more content online and are very susceptible to click-bait. How many times have you seen something on Twitter or Facebook, or at the bottom of the Huffington Post article you just finished reading, and clicked on it out of curiosity? Users may ignore your ads, but they'll click on your shared content, and if that content is on-brand and your website is user-friendly, chances are, they'll read much more once they get there.

CORPORATE AND COMMUNITY PARTNERSHIPS

One of the most fun and rewarding aspects of my job is the opportunity to think outside the box and come up with creative ways to market our authors. Many times, this includes getting involved with other businesses or community organizations.

By definition, partnerships are mutually beneficial. It's not just one person helping another. The key to getting corporations or community organizations to team up is to emphasize how the initiative will help them, not you.

When we started plans for *Running with the Devil* (the first book I worked on), we discussed doing a book trailer. As we addressed in the "Social Media" chapter, these previews for the book are expensive, difficult to distribute, and generally aren't worth the return on investment. But we decided that if we could find a way for a company to sponsor the trailer and promote it through their channels, then it would be worth the time and money to execute it. Since the main character is an ultramarathon runner, our first stop was running shoe and apparel companies. After reaching out to the big guns

(Nike, New Balance, etc.) we successfully connected with Sugoi, a smaller, but popular, fitness apparel company.

The pitch didn't include all the ways we needed their help. Instead, I focused on Jamie's brand and how aligning their company with her would help them in the long run. A runner herself, Jamie would be connecting with other runners to promote her book, and the Sugoi connection would increase their brand awareness. We also offered a box of books that the reps could give as gifts to their biggest accounts—a nice gesture of appreciation on their part as well as a way to build buzz for the book. Once they saw how we would help them, they were more willing to help us. In the end, they sponsored the trailer, posted it on their corporate site, and reviewed the book on their blog. All of these initiatives cost them very little, and both parties benefited from the increased exposure and opportunity to reach a new audience.

With every author, we try to think of companies or organizations who may benefit and be open to partnering for cross promotions. We've managed to secure successful partnerships with Blick Art Supplies, Lurie Children's Hospital, CheapOAir, and others. The first step, as always, is to think of your target audience. Then, think about the hooks in your book that align with companies, products, or organizations that reach your target audience. One of our authors wrote a book called *The Dog Park*, so we partnered with area pet stores for events and hosted a table at a PAWS run. Dog lovers tend to enjoy reading books featuring dogs, so these events reached our target audience. If your book is about landing your first job, consider teaming up with area colleges or recruiting agencies. If your protagonist has some sort of disability or has recovered from an illness, seek out nonprofits that benefit people with those disabilities or illnesses. As long as there is a clear hook and the opportunity to reach your target audience, it's worth a shot.

While it's always worth trying the bigger companies, I wouldn't hold your breath. I've had numerous conference calls with companies like Apple or Bloomingdale's trying to secure a partnership, and while they never led to anything, it was worth trying and at least we made the connection. Oftentimes, the smaller companies and start-ups are more open to experimenting with fresh ideas, and there are fewer hoops to jump through. When you create your list of companies and organizations to contact, I recommend pulling together a mix of large, medium, and small. The large companies may take more time and energy to get through to, but if they get on board, it's well worth it.

ADVERTISING

I've touched on advertising a bit throughout the book in the context of social media and online platforms, but since it's a part of so many promotional campaigns, I feel it demands its own section.

Many authors and publishers choose to focus more on advertising than media coverage, and in some ways, I understand why. Unlike media, which is never a sure thing, advertising is pay-to-play. If you pay for the placement, you get it. It's a guarantee. But unlike media coverage, where readers actually read the articles and absorb the information, advertising is often tuned out, an image or graphic given only a second of attention. People need to see or hear something multiple times before it sticks in their memory, and while I believe it only takes three or four media placements to do the trick, advertising alone requires 7–10 impressions before it sticks.

There are many different types of advertisements:

- Print ads (magazine and newspaper)
- Radio and TV spots (read by the host or a produced commercial)
- Display ads (online)
- Pay-per-click advertising (only pay when someone clicks)
- CPM (cost for displaying the ad 1,000 times, or impressions)

All of these are clearly defined as advertisements. You write the script or create the graphic and the message, and it's clear to the consumer that it's a sales tool. A compelling, well-placed ad can make an impression, but since you have to make so many impressions for someone to remember the product, these ads often aren't worth the return on investment. Furthermore, if an ad campaign isn't also complemented by a nationwide publicity campaign, then the rate of people who see your ad and actually buy your book goes way down.

Another type of advertisement is called an advertorial. This is a blend of advertising and editorial where a company or individual pays for editorial coverage. It's written by someone on staff, using the same editorial format as the rest of the publication. Advertorials can be in magazines and newsletters, and even television shows are doing paid spots. Unlike traditional advertisements that people quickly identify as advertisements, advertorials are often mistaken for editorial coverage, which makes a longer lasting impression. You have to look closely and read the fine print to see that it's paid placement, and most people don't take the time to do that.

There is no substitution for media coverage when it comes to making an impression, but if you're unable to secure that coverage, advertorials can be the next best thing. Those worth doing aren't necessarily cheap, but if you have the budget and want to dedicate a portion of it to advertising, I'd spend money on this over a similar-priced display ad.

I could spend an entire book evaluating various forms of advertising and identifying which ones are worth it and why, but that's not the focus of this book. Our focus is on building your author brand. While advertising can be a great complement to your other initiatives, advertising alone doesn't build a brand. Think about your other publicity and marketing initiatives and consider ways you can reach that audience again through forms of advertising. If you're executing a YouTube campaign, then securing some pay-per-click advertising with YouTube and other social media channels could tip the scales in your favor. If you're targeting women's magazines and have a bigger budget, then an advertorial with PureWow or another women's lifestyle publication could make a difference. Advertising should serve you by making additional impressions, not the only one.

THE PRICING GAME

In recent years, one of the most effective ways to build an audience for an established author is to play around with prices of e-books. All successful self-published authors will tell you that pricing plays a key role in the success of the book. If you're a debut author with a traditional publisher, e-book pricing strategies may not have the same effect. But if you're self-publishing or have multiple books out with a traditional publisher, pricing is an important factor to consider when it comes to attracting new readers.

What Should E-Books Cost?

For those of you with an extensive backlist, I recommend graduated e-book pricing. Let's say you have a series of five books: I recommend placing the first one as free. Readers are risk averse, but if you write quality books and a compelling series, you will hook readers from Book One. The next two in the series should be listed at $3.99. This is slightly higher than "sale price" e-books, but still cheap enough that readers won't think too much about purchasing them. Book Four should be listed at $4.99 and book five at $5.99. By the time readers are on the fourth and fifth books, they've committed to the series and won't mind paying the higher prices for the most current books.

Nonfiction is a bit different. Even if you've written multiple books, they're usually not a part of a series, and if they are, readers don't devour a series of nonfiction books in the same way. Because there are so many different genres and subgenres of nonfiction, I recommend doing market research to see how things are priced. Keep in mind the length of the book and whether it is self- or traditionally published. Shorter books are often priced lower, traditionally published books are usually priced higher, etc. Look at the books similar in subject, length, and type of publisher, and place your book somewhere in the middle. If books in your category range from $3.99–$12.99, then I recommend pricing around $5.99.

Discounting E-Books

If you're with a traditional publisher, you have limited control over pricing. It can be frustrating for many authors to have a $12.99 e-book that simply won't sell. Most publishers won't budge on the list price of an e-book, but they may be open to running a sale or discount promotion to build an audience for your frontlist. Some examples include:

DISCOUNTED PREORDER PRICE: When you preorder a print book from an online retailer, it's usually discounted from the normal retail price, so why wouldn't it be the same for e-books? Some publishers have become more open to down-pricing the e-book while it's available for preorder, then raising the price on the pub date. If the e-book is normally $11.99, but preordering will only cost $7.99, it incentivizes readers to order early and boost numbers the week the book goes on sale.

DISCOUNTING BACKLIST TITLES: If your publisher isn't open to negotiating the retail price of your e-books, they may be open to discounting one or two of them for a limited time.

If you write a series and you have a new one coming out, then I recommend discounting Book One in the series a couple months before. This will attract new readers and get them hooked on the series before the latest installment is available. If your books normally retail at $9.99 or higher, then I recommend discounting the first one to $2.99. If your books retail for less, then push for $0.99. Again, you'll have less say with a traditional publisher, but it never hurts to ask.

BUNDLE DISCOUNT: In our instant-gratification culture, many readers like to read multiple books in the series or all three books in a trilogy at one time. This mirrors the trend in binge-watching an entire television show season (or series) all at once instead of in weekly episodes. Rather than reading one book a year when they come out, some would rather wait and read all the installments at once. To attract these readers, many publishers will sell a collection of e-books and price it less than buying each individually. Not only does this allow you to move more books at one time, it also gives you a new product to sell without writing anything new.

E-Book Promotions

Reducing the price of your e-book isn't enough to attract new readers. You have to let those readers know that your book is on sale. You can (and should) promote the sale price through social media, but you're just reaching your current readers, not new ones. Fortunately, the rise of e-books also brought about a rise in different ways people find out about new and sale-priced e-books.

The primary way readers find out about sale-price

e-books is through newsletter subscriptions. These newsletters include BookBub, Book Gorilla, and Riffle Select.
There are probably more, but these are the ones we have the
most experience with and have found to be effective. They
all work the same way: you pay to have your discounted
e-book included in their daily e-blast and on their website.
The cost varies depending on the newsletter, and the cost is
directly related to the number of subscribers.

BookBub is by far the most expensive, ranging from $55
for the smaller lists (Parenting, Dark Erotica) all the way up
to $2,300 for the various mystery lists. However, they have,
by far, the largest reach. Their top mystery list reaches over
3 million readers, and even their smaller lists reach hundreds
of thousands. Because they have the largest reach, BookBub
can also be the most competitive, depending on which list
you're submitting for. For every book that gets accepted for
a promotion, there are dozens more that don't make the cut.
Having a decent sales record and lots of positive reviews,
along with submitting to the appropriate list, will better your
chances of being selected.

Riffle has a smaller subscriber list, around 100,000
depending on the list, and therefore doesn't have the same
impact. However the cost is only $25–$100 depending on
the genre, so even if it makes a small impact, it can be worth
the return on investment. Book Gorilla falls in the middle,
both in terms of subscribers and costs.

There are also numerous websites and blogs that post
e-book discounts. Most of these sites don't charge to be
listed, but since it's editorial, they won't list every book that's
submitted. However, it's free to submit, so it's worth a shot!

The last, and sometimes most effective, way to market
e-book discounts is through the online retailers. Amazon,

Barnes and Noble, iBooks, and Kobo all have a vested interest in promoting discounted e-books since they benefit from the uptick in sales just as much as you do. Most of the retailer promotions—Kindle Daily Deal, B&N Free Friday, etc.—are secured by traditional publishers and are highly coveted since they make such an impact. If you're with a traditional publisher, I recommend asking if they will be putting you up for any of these promotions. If you're self-published, it can be more difficult, but not impossible. Since it's based on how well the retailer thinks your book will sell, having a strong sales record and many positive reviews will help tip the scales. There are also a few distribution companies made specifically for self-published authors that work with the retailers to secure these types of placements. As your distributor, they'd receive a cut of every sale, paying a cut of something is better than receiving all of nothing.

When it comes to getting the most out of your sale-price e-book, more is more. Don't just go for one e-book newsletter—submit to all. Promote the sale on social media and submit the deal to the retailers for special promotions. The more you can get the word out about the book, the better the book will sell and continue to sell, even after it returns to its normal retail price.

This is only a small sampling of the marketing tools available to authors, but they're a great place to start. Are you considering one that isn't included here? I'm a strong believer in trying new things, as long as those things reach your target audience and aren't so cost prohibitive that you could never really earn a return on your investment. Experiment with new things and get creative, but make sure to do your research first and always evaluate your end results.

SAMPLE CAMPAIGN

Now that we have covered all the various pieces of the branding process—traditional media, online media, social media, events, and additional marketing opportunities—you'll need to map out a plan to string them all together. You have the tools necessary to play an active role in the branding process and successfully market you and your book. But like a contractor, your tools are useless without a concrete plan.

While you've done some of this as you read—coming up with a branding strategy, a media list, etc.—it's important to take a step back and get a clear sense of what your overarching campaign will look like, and what results you expect to yield. I recommend creating a publicity file that will hold the following:

- Outreach calendar (tasks you plan to complete and by what date)
- Media lists
- Event lists

- Social media content strategy
- Ideas for additional promotion (corporate sponsorships, online contests, etc.)
- Press materials

These should all be compiled well in advance of publication. Once you've created these materials, look over everything and ask yourself the following questions:

- What is my goal for this book, and do these initiatives help me reach that goal?
- Do these initiatives reach my target audience?
- Is everything—press materials, event lineup, and outreach list—on brand?
- Looking at the outreach calendar, is it possible to execute everything myself or do I need to hire someone else?

If you've followed the guidelines in the previous chapters, the answers to the first three questions should be yes. The last one will depend on your work schedule and writing demands. You may not have the budget to hire a whole PR firm, but there are virtual assistants, social media consultants, and other people who can alleviate the workload without draining your budget. Identifying whether or not you'll need help up front will prevent you from taking on too much and frantically trying to find help at the eleventh hour.

I've always been a visual learner, and I understand concepts best when I can see examples. With that in mind, I'm including examples of each document you should compile prior to beginning your outreach campaign:

SAMPLE OUTREACH CALENDAR

FEBRUARY

- Pitch long-lead outlets
- Update website and implement social media suggestions
- Begin scheduling any events around launch

MARCH

- Follow up with all long-lead outlets
- Finalize event schedule
- Begin compiling mailing list (fans, friends, family)

APRIL

- Pitch short-lead outlets
- Follow up with short leads 10–14 days after initial pitch
- Send out newsletter—include info about the book, any blurbs, links to preorder, and event schedule

MAY

- Pitch all online outlets
- Follow up with online outlets 7–10 days after initial pitch
- Follow up with anyone who requested a book or expressed interest

JUNE (LAUNCH MONTH)

- Final follow-ups
- Promote launch via social media
- Send out launch day newsletter

Depending on how busy you are, you may want to map out specific days or weeks to execute each of the tasks on hand. Otherwise, this can simply serve as a checklist of items that need to be executed by the end of each month. If you want something more sophisticated than a Word doc, I recommend using task managers like Todoist and Toodledo, which will allow you to create projects, tasks, and due dates.

SAMPLE MEDIA LIST

First Name	Last Name	Outlet	Notes
Jacqualine	Bach	*ALAN Review*	
Tina	Donvito	ASTROgirl	
Deb	Rochford	*AzTeen Magazine*	Needs local hook
Tracy	Kay	*Bleech*	
Naomi	Davis	Book Geek Confessions	
Allison	Hammond	*BookPage*	
Perizae	Tzantarmas	*BYOU Magazine*	
Sarah	Verney	*Discovery Girls*	
Erin	Gross	Fangirlish	
Dana	Krook	*Faze* magazine	Reviewed previous title
Kim	Childress	*Girls' Life*	
Margaret	Udovc	*Girlworks*	
Melissa	Hartman	Imagine	
Bill	Lieberman	*J-14*	
Julie	Weaver	*Justine*	

First Name	Last Name	Outlet	Notes
Natalie	Higdon	*M-Teen Magazine*	
Rachael	Cain	*New Expression*	
Morgan	Packard	*New Orleans Magazine*	Local author hook
Kim	Hubbard	*People*	
Alexandra	Abel	*Seventeen*	
Sheila	Sampath	*Shameless Magazine*	
Jennifer	Jhon	*South Florida Sun Sentinel*	
Dana	Mathews	*Teen VOGUE*	
Amy	Robinson	*The Charleston Gazette*	Pitch November event
Cheryl	Taylor	*The Mind's Eye Newspaper*	
Patricia	Smith	*New York Times* "Upfront"	
Tina	Donvito	*Twist*	
Lisa	Kurdyla	*VOYA*	Reviewed previous book
Lucia	Tran	*Zooey Magazine*	

These are all long-lead outlets. On your spreadsheet, you should have tabs for short-lead media, bloggers, and any guest articles you plan to pitch. Ideally, the media will be separated by the time you plan to pitch them. As you can see here, there are a few daily newspapers and online outlets, but these are critics who need a longer lead time, and therefore, will be pitched to sooner.

SAMPLE EVENT LIST

Venue	Location	Contact	Notes
Diesel Bookstore	Brentwood (LA)		Local launch party
B&N in San Jose	San Jose, CA		Hometown launch event
La Crescenta Women's Club	Pasadena, CA		Book group
Temecula Valley Women's Club	Temecula, CA		Book group
Tucson Festival of Books	Tucson, AZ		Submit in July
LA Times Festival of Books	Los Angeles, CA		Publisher is submitting
Cerritos Public Library	Cerritos, CA		Library group

The contacts are omitted to protect the organizers' privacy, but this is where you'd include the names and emails of the people you're planning on contacting.

SAMPLE SOCIAL MEDIA STRATEGY

We deliver online presence evaluations for all our authors. We go through all of their online platforms and provide suggestions on how to improve, what type of content they should be posting, and how they should network. The following is part of an evaluation for an author who writes police procedurals set in Oakland:

Twitter

- Increase posting to 3–5 times a day. You can utilize sites like HootSuite and TweetDeck to schedule tweets ahead of time.
- Increase the amount of interaction with other users. Make it a goal to @ reply or RT at least twice a day. This interaction should expand beyond talking with fellow authors. Instead, seek out media folks, booksellers, librarians, and bloggers. Network with people who will help spread the word about the book.
- Additional content can include:
  - Tidbits, photos, and articles about being in law enforcement
  - Photos and articles from the Bay Area, particularly Oakland
  - Tidbits from the writing process
- As you near the launch of XXX, increase the amount of promotional posts to 3 per week. These should consist of:
  - Links to positive reviews
  - Quotes from the book

- Link to read an excerpt
- Upcoming events or other news
- Avoid any straight "buy my book" tweets
- Utilize pertinent hashtags (#amwriting, #FridayReads) to increase discoverability.

Facebook

- Post 3–5 times a week following the suggested content from above.
- Whenever you post external links, I recommend including additional content or commentary so it's not just a link and a headline. This will entice people to click.
- Once you have an author page, you'll want to increase the number of "likes" that you have for other pages, this includes libraries, bookstores, media outlets, etc., that reach your potential reading audience.
- Discoverability increases with interaction, so post content that encourages comments, likes, and shares. Also, the more people click on your posts, the higher it shows up on newsfeeds.

RESULTS

The following materials are from an actual campaign we worked on a couple years back. By seeing the full range of the campaign, media secured, events planned, and social media platforms utilized, you will be able to outline your marketing plans for your own book.

Through all of this, the key point to remember is: know your audience. If a PR initiative doesn't reach your target audience, then it's not worth doing.

BOOK: *Control* by Lydia Kang
PUBLICATION DATE: December, 2013
DESCRIPTION: a debut YA sci-fi about genetic mutants, written by a practicing physician and mother of three
TARGET AUDIENCE: teens and parents of teens
TAGLINE: Michael Crichton for teens

TRADITIONAL PUBLICITY

RT Book Reviews (review publication featuring genre fiction) – review

VOYA (teen publication) – review

Omaha Magazine (local monthly magazine) – local author profile

Mom Talk Radio (syndicated radio show) – interview

KCMN with Tron Simpson (local radio) – interview

KAHI with Scott Costa (local radio) – interview

Omaha World Herald (local daily newspaper) – book feature

Writer's Digest (monthly magazine for writers) – debut author feature

The Morning Blend (local TV) – interview

ONLINE PUBLICITY

Huffington Post – Book Roundup

BuzzFeed – guest article

Went viral on social media, has received over 100,000 views to date

Mentioned on Creative Indie

Sunshine Reviews – review

Rally the Readers – review

Sirens of Suspense – interview

Addicted Readers – review

Late Nights with Good Books – review

Presenting Lenore – review

Sf Signal – review

Icey Books – review

Teen Writers Bloc – interview

The Reading Date – interview/review

Falling For YA – interview

Fiction Freak – review

Omaha.com – review

Good Books and Good Wine – review

EVENTS

Bookworm Bookshop, hometown launch event

Anderson's Bookshop, joint signing with Rachel Caine

St. Charles Public Library, YA author panel

Hazelwood Writers Week, talk and signing

Oak Creek High School, school presentation

Oak Creek Public Library, talk and signing

King Lab Middle School, school presentation

Chute Middle School, school presentation

826 Chicago, writing workshop

Chicago Comic and Entertainment Expo (C2E2), panel and signing

Philadelphia Science Festival, talk and signing

RT Booklovers Convention, panelist and YA day participant

SOCIAL MEDIA STRATEGY

- Focus on Twitter, Facebook, and Tumblr.
- Post content relating to science, medical advancements, thrillers, teen topics, and general pop culture content.
- Network with booksellers, librarians, and teachers who would spread the word about the book.
- Additional promotion through Wattpad. Lydia posted the first 5 pages on Wattpad.
    - For every 50 people who read the excerpt, Lydia revealed another 5 pages, up to 50 total pages.
    - Wattpad assisted with internal promotions, as did various authors on social media.
    - Penguin promoted the initiative through their social media channels.
    - The promotion ran in advance of publication to generate early buzz and build a fan base before the book came out.
    - To date, the excerpt has nearly 5,000 reads and 175 votes.

Overall, I viewed this as a successful campaign. We were able to establish her brand as an author, physician, and mother, and build a readership for the series. We secured coverage in a variety of mediums, all of which reached her target audience. The book may not have been reviewed in *Seventeen* or featured on TODAY as a top teen read, but getting a lot of coverage in smaller outlets can be just as effective as landing one big hit.

As you begin to secure media coverage for your own book, it's imperative that you keep a summary similar to this one.

It will help you track your success and identify key areas that are going well or that may be missing. You also want to have a record of coverage so that when you're ready to promote book two you know which outlets to target first.

In addition to recording media placements, you should also keep a record of which outlets passed, or asked for more information but never covered it. That way, you'll know who to leave off your list and who to contact with a reminder that they had expressed interest in your previous book. As I outlined earlier, the more detailed your record keeping, the easier it is to build relationships with media contacts. And the more data you have, the easier it is to gauge your success.

THE PROFESSIONALS

With this book and some dedicated time, you have the power to be your own publicist and launch a successful promotional campaign for your book. Many of the authors on the *New York Times* bestseller lists handle their own book promotion or only rely on the outreach of their in-house publicist. However, there are even more authors on that list who rely on the help of an outside professional.

IN-HOUSE VS. INDEPENDENT

As I outlined in the introduction, in-house publicists have many obstacles to overcome. They are usually responsible for promoting dozens of books each month without assistants or interns to help them with the some of the more tedious tasks. They are overworked and underpaid, and they can feel pressure from the higher ups because the fruit of their efforts is hard to quantify. It's a common joke that if the book tanks, you blame the publicist. If a book is a success, you praise the editor for finding the gem.

If you're assigned an in-house publicist by your publisher, you will have some support, but the question is: how much? Usually, what the in-house publicist is capable of doing on your behalf relates to the size of your advance and where you fall on his or her list of authors. Bigger advances mean your publisher made a bigger investment, which means they'll invest in the resources to promote the book effectively. If you receive a smaller advance, they won't have allocated the same budget to put into the promotion of your book. Additionally, some of it will depend on the media hooks in the book. If there's a lot to work with, an in-house publicist may be more inclined to go the extra distance.

In addition to an in-house publicist, you may also be assigned to an in-house marketing person or social media lead. The marketer will be responsible for things like advertising, giveaways, and corporate partnerships. A social media manager or coordinator would assist with building your online platform, promoting your work to social media influencers, and creating graphics to share across various platforms.

A key point to remember is that anyone who works for your publisher is exactly that: someone who works for your publisher. Their loyalty isn't to you, but to the book they acquired, and you are one of many, many books they publish each year. My clients tell me that one of the primary reasons they hired me is so they can have someone that's working for *them* and that will only act in their best interest.

Let's say you want to speak at the *Los Angeles Times*

Festival of Books. There are limited spots available and your in-house publicist has a short list of authors she or he is submitting. Not everyone is included on that list, and your in-house publicist won't always submit you just because you asked. The publicity team has identified the authors they want to push, and you won't always be one of them. However, your outside publicist works for you, and if you want to speak at the Festival, they can submit on your behalf.

These kinds of politics also come up when it comes to retailer-specific promotions. Publishers have a budget to spend with Amazon, Barnes and Noble, and independent retailers around the country. They are constantly trying to keep everyone happy and go to great lengths making sure one retailer isn't favored over another. Therefore, they may be less inclined to run a promotion through Amazon or anything that's retailer specific. But an outside publicist doesn't have to be concerned with internal politics and keeping the retailer accounts happy. They can do anything that will generate sales for the book.

The main takeaway about hiring an outside publicist is that they work for you and do not operate within the confines of a publishing house. With your publisher, you will be dealing with an in-house publicist, marketing person, sometimes a social media manager, or even a sales rep. An outside publicist can be your point person for these many contacts. Ideally, all of these roles should be intertwined and work together to form a cohesive campaign, but more often than not, all these individuals work in separate departments and don't always know what the other is doing. As an outside publicist, I am constantly filling in marketing on what publicity is doing, or sending recent media hits to the sales department so they can notify the booksellers. Promotional campaigns are most successful when all departments work together, so an outside publicist often plays a role in ensuring that happens.

When I talk to Big Five authors about the possibility of working together, nearly all of them ask me how the dynamic works between their in-house publicist and myself. Do they feel like their toes are getting stepped on? Does it result in them feeling like they're off the hook and may promote the book less?

In most cases, the answer is no. Nearly all the in-house publicists we've worked with are happy for the additional support. And rather than dropping everything and leaving all promotions to the outside publicist, they're more determined than ever to secure media coverage and make an equal contribution. Good publicists, inside and out, will work as teammates, not adversaries.

You may not have the budget for an outside publicist, and that's okay. After reading this book, you have the tools and knowledge to fill in any gaps. But whether you're hiring someone else or acting as your own outside publicist, it's important to understand everyone's role and figure out a plan for working together.

THE RIGHT QUESTIONS

If you're with a traditional publisher, they will assign you an in-house publicist. But if you're on your own, or want someone to supplement your in-house publicists' efforts, you'll need to find an outside publicist. When it comes to in-house publicists, you don't have much say in the matter, but it's important to ask plenty of questions and be informed of their plans. When looking for an outside publicist, there are hundreds of us, all with different styles, philosophies, and specialties. It's up to you to find the publicist that is the best for you and your project.

Whether you're heading into the marketing meeting at your publisher or interviewing someone on the outside, there are several questions you should ask:

Who Do You See as the Intended Audience for the Book?

Your publicist's primary role is to secure media coverage for you and the book, but if that media doesn't reach your target audience, it's not going to result in sales. You want to make sure the publicist understands the target audience and how best to reach them.

Some of this is a matter of opinion, so if they say they see your book being read by urban hipsters while you see it as more of a book club book, hear them out. They may have valid points. And if your in-house publicist wants to target the urban hipsters, you can probably find an outside publicist to hit up the book-clubbers.

What Is Your Pitching Process? How Do You Contact and Follow Up with Media Outlets?

As was outlined in the "Pitching" section, creating tailored pitches and diligently following up are key to securing review coverage. But there are many publicists who still send mass emails and don't follow up on leads. It's important to know which kind of publicist you're talking to.

For follow-ups, you want a publicist who's going to get on the phone. Many emails slip through the cracks and many radio producers don't even check their email. Following up via phone is an important component in ensuring your pitch gets noticed.

What is Your Timeline for the Campaign?

It's easy to get nervous and insecure when you don't know when things are happening. Having a loose outline of when certain outlets are going to be pitched, when a blog tour will be launched, when you can expect to see coverage, etc. will help put you at ease.

All publicists should have a timeline for their campaigns, and although that timeline may shift based on the news cycle, holidays, and other factors, it should give you an idea of what they're doing and when.

What is Your Communication Style?

You want to have a good working relationship with your publicist, and agreeing on a communication style is a key part of that. If your in-house publicist says she or he only emails when she gets a hit or prefers to do everything via email, then it's best to respect that. Also, letting your in-house person know that you're on email all day or that you're only available for calls later in the evening will help set the expectations so both of you can communicate more effectively.

If you're hiring an outside publicist, you want to find someone who gels with your communication style. If they don't do phone calls, but you are really more of a phone person, then that publicist isn't right for you. You also want to make sure they work well with your in-house team.

I find that the most frustrating working relationships are a result of poor communication and expectations that aren't grounded in facts. By asking the right questions up front, you are able to set appropriate expectations and have a clear line of communication, avoiding problems down the road.

THE RIGHT COMPANY

There are dozens of ways to effectively market a book, and for every possible marketing tool, there's an agency that specializes in it. There are publicists and PR companies that focus on many aspects of book promotion (publicity, marketing, social media) and there are others who specialize in one aspect of a promotional campaign. In some cases, it makes sense to hire someone who does it all, but if you have strong support from your in-house team in certain areas, then it may make sense to hire someone who specializes in other areas.

Traditional Media Only

As the pool of traditional media shrinks, so does the amount of PR firms who only handle traditional media. But they're still around. These companies specialize in traditional media placement and focus all their energy there. If your in-house team is focusing all their efforts online, or you're self-publishing and you feel comfortable with online media outreach, then it may make sense to enlist this type of company.

However, there are two caveats when it comes to hiring this type of publicist. The first is to think about your audience. Is traditional media the best way to reach them? Is there a reason your in-house team is focusing online? If your target readership doesn't consume traditional media, then it doesn't make sense to invest money in a traditional PR firm. The second is whether or not securing traditional media is realistic. Most book reviewers don't review self-published books, and unless you write nonfiction, it may be hard to book radio and TV as well. No PR company will guarantee media coverage, so it would be a shame to invest a lot of money without seeing any results. Additionally, traditional media doesn't tend to move the needle when it comes to e-book originals. If your book isn't available in print, or if it is but not widely distributed to bookstores, then traditional media may not make sense.

Remember, if the goal is to sell books, then you should invest your time and money in initiatives that will reach that goal. Traditional media really only works if that's how your target audience receives their information and if your book is on bookstore shelves nationwide.

Online Media Only

With the surge of websites and blogs, we've also seen a surge in online-only publicists. Some of these companies focus on blogger outreach only, while others execute more comprehensive online campaigns. As with everything, the key is knowing your audience and the best outlets to reach them. If your readers get all their information online, then it would make sense to work with an online-only publicist.

With these companies, the caveat lies in experience and approach. There are many bloggers who now call themselves "publicists" and will pitch your book to all their blogger friends. These amateur publicists are usually more affordable, but less effective and professional. Everyone has to start somewhere, so I'm never opposed to giving a new person a chance, but it's always a good idea to know their previous experience and to ask for references. If they've only worked on a handful of campaigns, but those authors were happy, then it's worth giving them a shot.

Online publicity companies often vary in their approach. I've seen proposals from companies that say they'll contact 1,000 bloggers or at least 500 online outlets. These trigger suspicion for two reasons. First, there is no way someone is writing 1,000 tailored pitch emails to these outlets. If they're contacting that many bloggers, it means they're using an email-blast format, which seldom yields the best results. Second, when they're pitching to that many outlets, how many of those outlets actually get a decent amount of traffic or are tailored to your specific book?

Our database consists of about 500 high-traffic blogs, and we comb through that database regularly to eliminate outlets that don't blog very often or whose content has decreased in quality. Does that mean we don't have the same reach as these other companies? Maybe. But it could also mean we're just more particular about who we put in our database.

Even with those 500 blogs, we don't contact every blogger for every book. We use our various filters to identify the top 30 or 50 who are most likely to give that book a positive review. As this book has outlined, a successful campaign is not about the quantity of reviews, but the quality, and not all online-only publicity companies share that philosophy.

Social Media Managers

Since the launch of Twitter and Facebook going public, the role of Social Media Manager has been in high demand. Everyone from celebrities to Fortune 500 companies to nonprofits have seen the need for an individual or a team to manage these various social media platforms and create a content strategy.

Most authors I talk to would be *thrilled* to turn their social media duties over to a professional and have them off their plate. There are many talented tweeters out there who have a solid understanding of social media strategy and capturing an author voice, but regardless of their talent, there is no substitution for authors posting themselves.

However, social media managers can work in a variety of ways. Some will be your voice and tweet, Facebook, etc. on your behalf. Others will assist you in crafting quality content, create graphics to accompany that content, and post at the optimal times throughout the day. Some will interact with other users, as you; others won't. There are also social media pros who only consult, going through your various online platforms and offering recommendations on how to make them better.

If you are a tech-zero or know that you will never, *ever* have an active social media presence, or are a huge bestseller who doesn't have time to manage their platforms, then hiring a professional makes sense. But if you have the capabilities to handle your own social media platforms, even if it's a pain and a chore, then I recommend sucking it up and doing it. If you need assistance, you can always hire someone to consult.

Marketing and Advertising Companies

If you feel that you and your in-house team have the publicity front covered and you have a budget to spare, then you may want to consider hiring a marketing or advertising company to assist with promotions. As was outlined in the previous section, there are many different marketing and advertising opportunities available to authors, and since these companies do it for a living, it may make sense to employ their help to ensure you're spending your money wisely.

The advantage to hiring these companies is that since they are buying ads and initiating campaigns for multiple clients, they often receive a discount or are able to get into promotions that have a higher minimum buy-in. For example, Amazon has a minimum ad buy of $10,000 per year. That's usually more than one author can afford. But if an advertising company is buying space for multiple authors, they can reach the minimum without passing along the entire cost to one author.

Additionally, most reputable companies have a clear understanding of what works and what doesn't. You may be interested in certain ad buys or marketing initiatives, but if those haven't proven effective, they'll let you know and recommend more appropriate places to spend your money.

That being said, there are certain reasons to be wary of marketing and advertising companies. First, you should understand that you're not only paying for the ad space, but you're also paying for their services. In some cases, you could place the ad yourself without the additional fee of a company. Second, because they work with vendors and have minimums to spend each year, some companies will attempt to sway you in a particular direction, even if it's not in your best interest. Again, reputable companies will let you know which ad buys are worth the investment, but other companies may be more loyal to their vendors than their clients.

The last caveat is to be wary of any company that is plug-and-play or offers one-size-fits-all packages. I've seen a number of companies that offer a shopping list of ad buys and marketing efforts that authors can sign on for, regardless of what makes sense for their book. If you're hiring a professional to assist with marketing and advertising, they should do more than just place an ad for you. They should be consulting on which initiatives make the most sense and steer you away from those that don't. Since every book is different, doing the same campaign for every book means a large percentage of their titles aren't being marketed appropriately.

Lecture Agents and Speakers Bureaus

Speakers Bureaus specialize in securing paid speaking engagements for clients. Their team of lecture agents are paid a commission for each engagement they secure, and while they usually focus on nonfiction authors and celebrities, a handful of fiction authors that use them as well.

Like hiring an outside PR or marketing company, the advantage to hiring a speakers bureau is that since this is their primary job, they have more contacts and better relationships with event coordinators and venues. And since they only take a cut of what they book, there's limited investment and risk on your part.

While the commission structure is appealing, it can also work as a disadvantage. Since it's in their best interest to book the client with the highest honorarium, most lecture agents are more focused on their celebrity, athlete, or media pundit clients. These are the folks bringing in $10,000 honorariums, sometimes more, so they'll push them before they'll push you. Additionally, since the speakers bureau assumes all the risk and initial investment, it can be difficult to get on their roster. Most authors have to work up to the larger honorariums on their own, or with the help of their publicity team, before applying to speakers bureaus, and even then, if they're on the lower end of the honorarium spectrum, they may not be getting booked as frequently as they'd like.

If speaking is something you want to do on a regular basis and have it be a part of your revenue stream, then I recommend seeking out potential speakers bureaus. There's no risk on your part, other than the time it takes to submit the application, and since most bureaus don't require exclusivity, you're able to apply to more than one and increase your chances for getting booked. However, if you haven't done any paid speaking engagements yet, I recommend starting smaller by booking things on your own and building up your résumé before taking the time to apply.

SEO Marketing

Search Engine Optimization (SEO) is a key when it comes to discoverability, so many businesses enlist companies to improve their SEO. There is no shortage of companies and individuals claiming to have the secret to boost SEO through a range of marketing techniques, keyword searches, and metadata.

I've talked to many authors, primarily in the nonfiction space, who are interested in hiring someone to boost their SEO and ensure their website shows up first in Google searches. And the conclusion I draw with every conversation is that these authors are looking for an easy way out. They want to throw money at the problem and be done with it, rather than relying on organic marketing techniques to boost their ranking.

When I first started freelancing, I wasn't showing up in Google searches. There was another Dana Kaye, a journalist who died of lung cancer, who would always show up on the first page. Searching for "Dana Kaye books" or "Dana Kaye book review" would produce my name, but a general search would push me to the second and third pages. However, the more I wrote, the more I published, and the more inbound links I received, the higher I climbed. Within a year, I was the first 5 entries in Google, and Dana Kaye the journalist was pushed to page two.

This didn't happen overnight. It took an active social media presence, regularly publishing, and generating inbound links to push me up in the ranks. And while there are companies who claim they can do it overnight, I believe Google is smart enough to recognize those tactics and will prevent them from working.

If you're concerned with your website and where it's showing up in searches, you can always hire a web developer or SEO specialist to offer a consultation. They'll be able to identify if there's anything wrong with your website or other factors that may be hurting you in searches. But more likely, they'll tell you what we've already outlined in this book: Google juice comes from generating inbound links, posting pertinent content, and updating your website on a regular basis.

WARNING SIGNS

Because there are so many agencies and individuals, specializing in a wide range of areas, it can be difficult to know which one is the best for you and will provide a return on investment. There are many talented publicists and marketers who care about the success of the book and have the experience and skills to deliver on their promises, but there are many more who will take on anyone who can cut a check, make promises they can't deliver on, or just don't have the skills and experience necessary to execute a solid campaign.

The tricky part about finding the right PR company is that most of them know how to pitch. I've lost out on contracts to publicists who promise the client the sun, moon, and stars, and have an engaging Powerpoint to go with it. We

pitch media for a living, and therefore, most publicists talk a good game and know what it takes to get a client to sign on the dotted line. But just because the publicist presents an impressive presentation and promises to deliver on any media you can think of, doesn't mean he or she is the right person.

So, when you interview publicists, I recommend paying attention to the following warning signs.

Guarantee of Media Placement

As we addressed in the "Traditional Media" section, securing media coverage is never a guarantee. You can have a great lineup of interviews and newspaper features booked, but if something huge happens in the world, your fluffy author piece is going to get bumped. No publicist can guarantee a certain amount of media coverage or placement in certain publications.

There are a handful of publicists I've met that work on a pay-per-interview basis. They are only paid when interviews or features are secured. Many authors find this appealing because, like lecture agents, there is minimal financial risk. However, like lecture agents, these publicists are going to focus their attention on the clients with the easy pitch. If they go out to a round of media contacts and no one bites, they're not going to invest more time chasing down those leads. They're going to move on to a client who's more media friendly, and you'll be left without any publicity for your upcoming book.

Guarantee of Hitting a Bestseller List

I know many authors who have spoken to other publicists who have guaranteed them they'd hit the *New York Times, USA Today,* or other bestseller lists, and I am still appalled when I think about this fact. Bestseller lists are a ranking system, and making those lists not only depends on the sales of your book, but the sales of everyone else's books as well. You can sell thousands of copies in a single week, but if 10 other books sell hundreds of thousands, then you're not making the list. On the flip side, I've seen books that sell less than a thousand copies make the list because it was a slow week in their category. There have been many authors (and a couple noted celebrities) who purchased large quantities of their own books in an attempt to tip the scales, and have still come up short.

Making a bestseller list is not up to one person. Anyone who guarantees you bestseller placement is making false promises, and I question their understanding of the industry. Run.

Unable to Provide References

Whenever anyone asks if they should hire anyone, whether it's a publicist, a web designer, or a handyman, my response is always the same: have you been able to find three people with similar projects who can vouch for them?

The best way to know if a publicist or marketer is reputable and will be able to do right by your book is if other authors are able to vouch for him or her. In the interview process, I recommend asking for three references, but not just any references—authors that are similar to you. A huge *New York Times* bestseller may have great things to say about his publicist, but that doesn't mean the person knows how to market a debut or a struggling midlister. Nonfiction authors don't make the best references if you write fiction, because the promotional process is so different. If three authors say that hiring this publicist was a good idea, and their books and goals are similar to yours, then it's indicative that this publicist would be a good fit for you. But just because you met one vocal author who vouches for a particular publicist doesn't necessarily mean they're the right fit for you.

As I mentioned previously, I do believe that everyone has to start somewhere. If you had contacted me in early 2009, I wouldn't have been able to provide three author references because I only had one client. If you are considering going with someone newer and more affordable, then I recommend asking for non-client references. Ask to speak to any in-house publicists, book critics, or producers he or she has worked with. If there aren't enough clients to vouch for services, media and publishing people can be the next best thing.

No Desire to Read Your Book

Before we take on any client, we must read their book. How could we possibly market something we haven't read? Additionally, we only take on a small percentage of the authors who query us, because the book may have a great marketing hook, but if I don't feel it's a good book or it just doesn't gel with my reading tastes, then I don't feel comfortable standing behind it. But I am continuously shocked at how many publicists say they don't need to read the book to offer a proposal.

As an author, you want to have a publicist that can get behind your book, understands the content, and ultimately, believes in the project. Your publicist should be able to understand your target audience and pull out "off the book page" marketing angles, but it's very difficult to do that without having read the book. Even advertising and marketing companies we've worked with say they want to read the book before offering a recommendation, because again, how can they know which ad buys will yield the best return on investment if they don't understand the target audience and secondary themes of the book?

When you interview publicists, take note of whether or not they ask to read your book prior to offering a proposal. If they don't, you can offer to send the manuscript and see what they say. If they don't express a need or even a desire to read your work, then I wouldn't trust them to promote it.

Whether or not you hire outside PR, marketing, or advertising does not determine the fate of your book. I am confident that by reading this book you have the necessary tools to execute an effective promotional campaign. But should you decide on hiring the professionals, it is key to ask the right questions, determine which type of company best fits your needs, and watch out for the warning signs before signing on the dotted line.

CONCLUSION

One of the most common questions I'm asked from potential clients is: "How do you gauge success?" Even though I'm asked this question frequently, I still find it difficult to answer.

The easy answer is sales. If your books are selling better than they did prior to the publicity campaign, then it's easy to consider your promotional efforts successful. But launching a bestseller is a lot like launching a missile: everyone—publicity, marketing, and sales—needs to turn their keys. There have been a few instances where we secured amazing national media coverage, built the clients' social media followings, and executed a handful of well-attended events, and the books still didn't sell in the way we had hoped. This is usually a result of the sales team not securing strong bookstore placement or not having a marketing budget. Does that mean the promotional campaign we executed wasn't successful? Not necessarily.

Even after working in this industry for nearly a decade, I am still an optimist. I believe that as long as there are readers, every quality book has the potential for success. The decline of traditional media, especially when it comes to book coverage, the surge of e-books being published, and the ever changing "rules" of social media can make book promotion more challenging. But if the book is well written and there are readers interested in the content, then with hard work and a solid strategy, I'm confident in its ability to sell.

Charlaine Harris, author of the Sookie Stackhouse series, which inspired the hit series *True Blood*, often jokes that she is a ten-year overnight success. Now, every book she writes hits the *New York Times* bestseller list, but that wasn't always the case. Did having a hit show help sell books? Absolutely. But she wouldn't have gotten that hit show if she didn't already have a solid fan base, positive publicity, and an established author brand.

In an ideal world, your publicity efforts would launch you onto bestseller lists the first time around, but the reality is, most authors don't break out with their first book. Bestsellerdom takes time, sometimes years, or in Harris's case, a decade.

To measure the success of a campaign, go back to your original goals. For most authors, the goal is to sell books. For others, it's to leverage speaking engagements, teaching positions, or other paid writing gigs. Now ask yourself, am I closer to that goal than I was before the campaign began? You may have not sold hundreds of thousands of books on the first try, but did you sell more than you would have had you done nothing? You may not be booking speaking engagements with $5,000 honorariums yet, but did you speak on a panel or teach a workshop pro bono so that you have something to put on your résumé or website? You may not have gotten a guest column or regular contributor spot yet, but did you secure an op-ed or guest interview that may lead to something more regular? You cannot measure each individual campaign by whether or not you achieved your end goal; instead, you must measure success by whether or not you moved closer to that end goal.

This book is not meant to be read only once. Since every book you publish will be slightly different, I recommend scanning these sections each time you gear up for a campaign. If you switch genres, or go between fiction and nonfiction, I recommend rereading with fresh eyes and the new project in mind. You will take away different ideas and aspects than you have this time around.

But no matter what you write, some key takeaways remain the same:

- Know your audience
- Stay on brand
- Be creative
- Have a plan

As an author, your primary job description is to write books. You are not a publicist, and therefore, book promotion should not make up for the majority of your day. It's easy to get caught up in all the things you *have* to do and become overwhelmed with all the marketing possibilities available to you. The purpose of this book is to outline and explain all the promotional tools you have at your disposal, and let you decide, based on your availability and target audience, which ones are most important to utilize. You do not need to do everything, nor do I think you should. It is far better to execute a few campaigns well than to focus on too many and execute them poorly.

Ultimately, this book is meant to empower you with information. Too many authors see marketing and publicity as something foreign and difficult to understand. In turn, these authors usually opt to not do anything to promote their books, or they attempt to ape other authors without any real goal or strategy in mind. Now that you have read this book and completed the exercises within, you have an overall understanding of the promotional process and what it takes to make your book a success.

I didn't go to school for communications, or work at a PR agency, or intern at a publisher. I learned how to effectively promote books through research and trial and error. If I can learn it, so can you. You've already taken the first step by reading this book: research. Now, the only thing left to do is try.

ACKNOWLEDGMENTS

I live my life by a Ray Bradbury quote: "Jump off the cliff and build your wings on the way down." I'd like to acknowledge those who chose to jump off the cliff with me.

First and foremost, none of this would be possible without my clients. They're the reason I look forward to work each day. They (for the most part) listen to my advice, let me run with my wild ideas, and ultimately, put their careers in my hands. A special thank you goes to Jamie Freveletti, who asked the question that started it all: why don't you just be my publicist?

To my talented colleague, editor, and most importantly, friend, Julia Borcherts. To all the interns who have shipped books, worked events, and created funny memes for our social media platforms.

To my amazing team at Diversion Books: Jaime Levine, Mary Cummings, Randall Klein, Nita Basu, and Sarah Masterson Hally. I feel so blessed to be working with such a talented, hardworking, and dedicated team.

To Barbara Poelle, Janet Reid, and Joanna Volpe for providing referrals, comic relief, and the much needed drink. They are some of the hardest working ladies in the business and I have such admiration for them.

To Jon and Ruth Jordan, for bringing me into the mystery community, into the castle, and into the family.

You're lucky to have one great parent, maybe two. I'm blessed to have six. To my amazing in-laws, Cheryl and Peter, for bringing me into the fold. To my Dad, who doesn't always understand what I do but encourages me anyway, and Leslie, who does understand and supports me in every way she can. To Judy, my fellow triathlete and small business owner, for always providing ears, insight, and plenty of cheering. And to Mom, whose love, patience, generosity, encouragement, and a whole lot of nudging made me the person I am today.

This book was written during naps and after bedtimes, so thank you to my amazing son for giving me the time to write without having to sacrifice a single moment with you. And finally for Nicole, who encourages me to reach for the stars while keeping my feet firmly planted on the ground.

DANA KAYE

is the owner of Kaye Publicity Inc., a boutique PR company specializing in publishing and entertainment. She received her B.A. in Fiction Writing from Columbia College Chicago. After college, she worked as a freelance writer and book critic. Her work has appeared in the *Chicago Sun-Times*, *Time Out* Chicago, *Crimespree Magazine*, *Windy City Times*, *Bitch Magazine*, and on GapersBlock.com. This experience has been crucial to her publicity career: she has the contacts and necessary industry insight to form pertinent, widespread media campaigns.

Dana is known for her innovative ideas and knowledge of current trends. She frequently speaks on the topics of social media, branding, and publishing trends, and her commentary has been featured on websites like The Huffington Post, Little Pink Book, and NBC Chicago.

For more insight into the publicity process, sign up for her newsletter (**bit.do/kayepublicity**) or enroll in one of her online courses (**kayepublicity.teachable.com**).